FDR's
UNFINISHED
PORTRAIT

FDR's
UNFINISHED
PORTRAIT

A Memoir by
Elizabeth Shoumatoff

University of Pittsburgh Press

Published by the University of Pittsburgh Press, Pittsburgh, Pa. 15260
Copyright © 1990, University of Pittsburgh Press

Baker & Taylor International, London

Manufactured in the United States of America

LIBRARY OF CONGRESS CATALOGING-IN-PUBLICATION DATA

Shoumatoff, Elizabeth.
    FDR'S unfinished portrait: a memoir/by Elizabeth Shoumatoff.
    p. cm.
    ISBN 0-8229-3659-3
    1. Shoumatoff, Elizabeth.   2. Portrait painters — United States —
Biography.   3. Watercolorists — United States — Biography.   4. Roosevelt,
Franklin D. (Franklin Delano), 1882–1945 — Portraits.   I. Title.
ND1839.S46A2   1991
759. 13 — dc20   90-39184
    [B]   CIP

Contents

Illustrations

Acknowledgments

Mrs. Zoric Ward, the eldest daughter of Elizabeth Shoumatoff, has been instrumental in several important preparatory stages of this book. In the dramatic episodes that followed her mother's return from Warm Springs in 1945, she had a vital role, as described in the text. Later, as the executor of her mother's will, she organized the files, including writings, photographs, and associated documents which form the basis for this book. In reading the final manuscript as well as the proofs, she made numerous contributions to its clarity and accuracy from her own memories of the family's early years and afterward. Mrs. Catherine Marshall, the managing editor of the University of Pittsburgh Press, compiled the final manuscript. She made the definitive selection and arrangement of the text and illustrations and gave extraordinary attention to details of the text and to checking of the facts and names. Without these contributions by Mrs. Ward and Mrs. Marshall, this book would not have been possible.

NICHOLAS SHOUMATOFF

Prologue

Among the artists of her time, Elizabeth Shoumatoff (1888–1980) was unquestionably one of the most productive and successful, but she never took part in what is known as the art world, or in any art movements. As a young woman in her native Russia, before coming to America in 1917 she painted her own family and friends as often as they, in her words, "had the patience to pose." Those early watercolor portraits have a haunting charm. They are small, with plain creamy backgrounds, and an incredibly smooth texture almost like that of a miniature. She also painted a few miniatures on ivory. Her later work, much of it in large dimensions and with richly colored backgrounds, is reminiscent of Romney and Gainsborough, even though it is almost all in the watercolor medium. The faces are rendered in the same fine texture as the earlier work, showing her subjects, as she said, at their best. In their total effect, they have a warmth entirely her own, which can be immediately recognized.

Before her marriage, Elizabeth lived with her father, General Nicholas Avinoff, her mother Alexandra, and her brothers Nicholas and Andrey, in a spacious and stately country house called Shideyevo, near Poltava in the Ukraine. It was also near Kharkov, where she was born. The house was not suitable for winter, which the family usually spent in St. Petersburg. The graceful quality of those early years, which resembled descriptions in Tolstoy's *Anna Karenina* and Chekhov's *The Cherry Orchard,* was reflected in all of Elizabeth Shoumatoff's work, and in all ninety-two years of her life.

After her arrival in America from Russia, adapting to the new country, which many found traumatic, was comparatively easy for her. This was partly because of her native optimism and durability, and partly because she grew up speaking English most of every day with her English governess, thus learning the language by instinct as only a small child can. The same governess also taught her how to paint in watercolors, which became the foundation for her remarkable career. She had a few other lessons but no formal art school training; she was essentially self-taught.

The transition from Russia, however, was not without trials, adventures, and narrow escapes as briefly mentioned in the following pages, and described in some detail by her grandson Alex in his book *Russian Blood.* The most traumatic part of it was a train ride across the endless Siberian *taiga,* with several interruptions by unruly or rebellious soldiers, during which her three-year old daughter Zoric, Elizabeth's only child at that time, was severely ill with pneumonia.

Elizabeth came to America with her husband Leo, who was on a mission for the provisional government headed by Alexander Kerensky that ruled Russia after the abdication of Tsar Nicholas in February 1917. This parliamentary government was overthrown later that year by Lenin's military coup. Today, with glasnost, even the Soviets openly acknowledge the short-lived and nonviolent "February revolution," which they so long tried to conceal by claiming that they overthrew the tsar; in fact, they were responsible for Russia's regressing from democracy to autocracy.

During the early years in the United States, after an unsuccessful attempt at farming in Pine Bush, N.Y., Elizabeth, Leo, and their three children, Sophie (Zoric Ward), Nicholas, and Elizabeth lived at Napanoch, N.Y., in a stately house with Ionic columns reminiscent of that childhood home in Russia. It was there, as she describes it, that Elizabeth's profession as a portrait painter really got underway.

Upon moving his family to Long Island in 1924, Leo became secretary, treasurer, and business manager of the Sikorsky Aviation Corporation, which built the first amphibian Clippers for Pan American Airways. Those were exciting times, during which legendary early flyers were frequent visitors at the Shoumatoff household. However, in one of the Sikorsky company's difficult first years, there was not enough money for the December payroll, whereupon Elizabeth gave the proceeds from one of her portraits to provide each factory worker with $10 for Christmas, almost a week's wages in those days. In 1928, Leo died in a drowning accident off Jones Beach. Elizabeth then had to support and educate her family by her painting.

Some of her subjects posed at her home or studio, and she often worked alone late at night. Mostly, however, as she much preferred to do, she painted people in their own homes, often as a house guest, where she could see them as their normal selves at ease in their usual surroundings. Her little watercolor paint box, less cumbersome than oil paints, was convenient for this purpose. Thus, in the years that followed, she became an extensive traveler. Not only her portraits, but also Elizabeth herself, were often seen in homes from Bar Harbor to Palm Beach, from Cape Cod, Newport, and Sea Island to Wyoming, Texas and Hawaii; she was especially well known in Wilmington, Baltimore, Washington, Winston-Salem, Atlanta, Pittsburgh, and Akron, as well as in Long Island and

New York. Her work is a unique record of a noteworthy but private segment of American life. She also painted in Canada, England, Belgium, Luxembourg, Italy, and Liberia.

Because of her keen interest in others and her great vitality, many of her subjects became close, lifelong friends. She often painted every member of a family, in a process which someone compared to measles. In several families, she painted three or four generations, and in one—the Frick family—she painted five generations. For the Firestone and du Pont families, and for the Woodruffs of Atlanta, she was virtually a "court painter." During sixty-three years in America, from 1917 to 1980, she produced more than two thousand portraits. This extended body of work resulted from "contagion" within families and among friends, from portraits seen in homes and by word of mouth. She had no agents or gallery connections, and during her lifetime she had no "one-man show." She truly abhorred publicity, an attitude which aided her success in painting people who wished to stay out of the gossip columns.

By far the most fateful of her trips occurred in 1945. She had been staying at a guest cottage of the Little White House at Warm Springs, Georgia, painting her second portrait of President Franklin D. Roosevelt from life (the first was in 1943). Shortly before lunch on April 12, 1945, while simultaneously working and posing, he addressed to her an apparently casual, but in retrospect moving remark, which proved to be his prophetic last words: "We have fifteen minutes more to work." Shortly afterward, he collapsed from a fatal cerebral hemorrhage. Only two other persons, at first unaware of what happened, were then in the room: his cousin Margaret Suckley, and his friend Mrs. Winthrop Rutherfurd.

Many volumes have been written about the last days of FDR, mostly by people who were not there and who copied each other's erroneous surmises. Elizabeth Shoumatoff's story, presented here, is the only authentic, firsthand account of FDR's last conscious moments. Her account is based on notes that she wrote during those days (other parts of this book were still being written during the very last year of her life.)

The remarkable unfinished portrait, one of her finest, shows FDR with a poignant spiritual expression. Describing it, she wrote that "to paint a portrait is to discern the essence of the soul . . . and even in that last portrait of FDR there has been recaptured something characteristic of his youth that had been carried through life, and sometimes is more expressive as life approaches its summation." No brush stroke has been added to that portrait; it remains a historic document of the last conscious minutes of FDR's life. It was donated by Elizabeth to the Warm Springs Foundation and now stands as a unique, permanent memorial to one of our greatest presidents, on an easel next to the armchair where he sat. A finished version of it is also at Warm Springs.

For many years after that traumatic experience, Elizabeth avoided painting heads of state. Finally, in 1956, she broke the spell and made a memorable trip to Liberia, where she painted a life-size portrait of President William V. S. Tubman. She also painted a posthumous portrait of FDR for the White House that was unveiled by President Lyndon B. Johnson at a reception in the East Room, which was really a reunion of surviving New Dealers and Roosevelt family members, with a reading by Charlton Heston from *Sunrise at Campobello.*

Later she painted the official White House portrait of President Johnson, which was made into a US postage stamp, and of Mrs. Lady Bird Johnson; she also painted their children and grandchildren and several more portraits of LBJ himself.

These paintings brought Elizabeth into close contact with the gracious first lady who has been a powerful influence in treasuring America's environment, and with the president who, a Southerner, pushed through and signed the Voting Rights and Civil Rights acts that finally ended legal apartheid in the United States, one hundred years after the Civil War. These presidential portraits, and a few others in various museums and institutions, are the only Shoumatoff paintings that can normally be seen by the public.

Elizabeth often spoke of the help she received from her brother Andrey Avinoff, who was director of the Carnegie Museum of Natural History in Pittsburgh and also a master artist, especially of flowers, butterflies, and landscapes. Until his death in 1949, he was her most effective teacher, sharpest critic, and often unmerciful teaser. Elizabeth had a lovely and clear soprano voice, and Andrey, a talented pianist, accompanied her in Ukrainian, Russian, French, and English folk songs which unfortunately were never recorded.

With a strong family tradition in the Russian Orthodox religion, even briefly intending, in her early youth, to become a nun, Elizabeth said she accomplished her work only through her faith in God. In her studio she had a framed image of St. Alypius, an early icon painter, showing him on his deathbed next to an unfinished icon on an easel; an angel stands before it with brush in hand, finishing the icon for him. After Elizabeth died, a small piece of paper was found on which she had written: "I am glad that I lived my long life in a world where there were spiritual values, beauty, and dignity."

NICHOLAS SHOUMATOFF
March 1990

FDR's
UNFINISHED
PORTRAIT

CHAPTER ONE

How It Started

Some time ago, in thinking about different events in my career as a portrait painter, I realized how fortunate I was. What a life! What a wonderful life it was! To have had the opportunity to paint so many interesting people, some quite extraordinary, others just delightful and often amusing; to know them so well and later to enjoy their friendship. What could be more exciting and gratifying? But somehow, as a little girl who lived on that old estate in Southern Russia, I knew it would happen. I dreamed that some day I would become another Elizabeth Vigée-Lebrun and like her, my ideal of those days, paint portraits of famous people. That dream did come true, but not until catastrophic events uprooted the very foundations of my life, engulfing everything that was connected with it.

My first steps in art began in the lovely surroundings of a beautiful old house on my mother's estate in southern Russia in the province of Poltava. Shideyevo was a typical mansion of the early part of the nineteenth century, with white columns and a cupola. It was located on an elevated ridge, the right bank of the river Orel, and the view from the terrace was breathtaking.

My great grandfather, Andrey Fyodorovitch Lukianovitch, participated in the Finnish war of 1809 and in 1820 became governor of the province of Simbirsk. When he started building the Shideyevo house, he had most of the lumber brought from there. The plans were made by Korinfsky, the same architect who built the Tauride Palace in St. Petersburg, which later became the Duma. According to his preliminary plans (they had been preserved and I remember seeing them), the building was to be much more elaborate, with a belvedere and four wings instead of two. But as it was, it presented a very impressive sight, and among the houses in the southern estates it could only be compared with Dikanka, the house of the Kotchubeys. Like the latter, one wing was a private church that was a copy of the Church of the Imperial Stables in St. Petersburg, famous for its simple classical lines.

Though destroyed long ago, at the time of the Revolution, that beloved house remains in my memory as vivid in every detail as the day I saw it for the last time. One of its most remarkable features was a collection of paintings originally acquired by my maternal great grandfather, Vladimir Panayeff, who was assistant secretary of the Imperial Court and closely connected with the Hermitage. Portraits of my ancestors covered the walls of the big hall, and in the drawing room hung a magnificent portrait by Levitsky of Catherine the Great, one of Empress Anne, paintings by Dutch artists (such as Teniers *fils*), one later identified as a Memling, and portraits of some eighteenth-century statesmen and generals.

Our family then consisted of my father, a general who was stationed for a few years in Tashkent, where we also stayed for a year, my mother, and two brothers, Nicholas and Andrey. Andrey, five years my senior, was remarkably gifted in every way. He was a scientist and an entomologist. Butterflies were his main interest. He played the piano beautifully, and his eloquence in making public addresses was outstanding, particularly when he later became the director of the Carnegie Museum of Natural History in Pittsburgh. His sense of humor in making cartoons of people was delightful. But what I really think he missed in life was a career as an artist; only after his retirement from the museum did he really devote himself to art. It was his influence and his merciless but constructive criticism that helped me more than anything with my work.

As long as I remember, I have had a pencil in my hand. In fact, one of the most vivid impressions of my early childhood was making the outline of something like a bird. I wanted to repeat it and was unable to do so. It was time to go to bed, which was the last thing I wanted. However, with tears and protestations I was laid in my crib.

The next thing was drawing noses and finally making a whole profile. It was always a human face that I wished to do.

When I was seven, my parents engaged an English governess, Frances B. Whishaw. A cultured and talented woman, she very soon began teaching me the rudiments of watercolor technique. I began painting on a real artist's block of rag paper. First, an earthenware pot with difficult reflections, and next a Chinese doll. It was quite exciting, particularly when I had to do the bright, beady, black eyes. That was my first portrait in watercolor, and from then on I did not stop. At the age of nine I got a rather good likeness of the nursery maid, Sasha, sitting on a chair, and at ten did a profile of my mother which made me quite proud. But I felt I could not be a real artist unless I painted in oils. With the exception of a few charming watercolors of ancestors, all the portraits I saw were in oils—including those of Mme. Vigée-Lebrun. An eighteenth-century French artist who had specialized in aristocratic portraiture, she was my chief inspiration at that time.

So when, at the age of fourteen, I started my instruction in oils with a private teacher, a young man from an art school, I felt I had reached the right medium and was really established in art. However, I received two rebuffs, the first when I was about seventeen. I painted a plein-air picture of a Ukrainian peasant girl holding a bunch of lilacs and proudly presented it, in a gilt frame, to my sister-in-law, Masha, as an anniversary gift. The house where it was to go was one of the most enchanting in Moscow, in exquisite taste to the last detail. The expression of dismay on Masha's face found its reflection in mine as I glanced at the lovely surroundings that combined the elegance of the Russian eighteenth century with English cheerfulness.

She gently suggested that next time I wanted to paint something for her she would love to have a copy of Peter Sokoloff's portrait of her grandmother. This artist was a famous portraitist of the beginning of the nineteenth century, and his lovely small paintings were a mark of good taste and respectability. As I began copying the oval picture of the beautiful woman in the purple velvet dress, I was entranced with his technique and delicate skin tones. I could not wait to do one of my mother exactly the same way, and then others followed, all in watercolor. What a joy I experienced! How grateful I am to Masha, who happened to be the channel to my present work.

The second confirmation of my inability to paint decent portraits in oils came somewhat later. Even though I was beginning to feel very free with my small watercolors, I still continued my private lessons in oils together with some friends. I was painting a girl of my acquaintance who posed as our model. It was a life-size canvas. She wore a velvet dress and a big picture hat with plumes. I thought it was rather magnificent until a very famous Russian art connoisseur and collector, Mr. Khanenko, saw it. He looked at it and then glanced at a recent watercolor I had done of my mother.

"You stick to your watercolor," he said quietly, "that is your medium."

And I knew then that he was right. But there was not much painting after that in either medium. After my marriage a few months before World War I began, came the shattering events that destroyed our world and tore us from our beloved country.

In the fall of 1917 we moved to the United States. The Provisional Government headed by Alexander Kerensky, which governed Russia immediately after the February Revolution, had appointed my husband as a representative of the Ministry of Supplies. My brother Andrey was already in America, sent by the Zemsky Union to buy supplies for the Russian war effort. Because of the fighting in Europe, we traveled by way of Siberia and across the Pacific Ocean. It was while we were in Hawaii that we learned of the second revolution that put the Communists in power. Nicholas, my oldest brother, who was assistant secretary of the interior, remained in Russia. He was arrested in 1937 and we never saw him again although Masha, his wife, later came to America, where she lived with me and in 1968 published her memoirs, *Marie Avinoff: Pilgrimage Through Hell*, by Paul Chavchavadze.

I cannot tell how distressed I was at the thought of living in America, which at that time meant only skyscrapers, dollars, and gangsters to me. Moreover, our sources of income were severed, and we would have to find new ways to support ourselves. After two dismal years of readjustment, we landed on an old farm near Pine Push, New York, which we managed to buy with what money was left. The family then consisted of my husband Leo and myself, our two small children Sophie (Zoric) and Nicholas, my mother, and Andrey.

How did I get back to my painting from this unpromising situation? This is a real story, that began in the most unforeseen way and developed like a unique pattern, bringing me the opportunity to paint people whom I hardly thought I could ever meet.

As it happened, the artist George Inness, Jr., and his family lived at a very close distance from us, on the crest of the narrow Shawangunk range, just south of the Catskill Mountains. His name already meant a great deal to me; in our few months of living in New York I had learned a little about American art. Somehow he heard about us and we were invited to visit.

Mrs. Inness was very big and not exactly beautiful, although her husband often referred to her as "my beautiful Julia." At that time Mr. Inness was a man in his sixties, not very tall, particularly next to his wife, slightly bald with a little gray moustache. He was the quintessence of charm, kindliness, and humor, as well as a remarkable storyteller. He later told me about his romance with Julia. He rendered it with so much charm and humor that I will always remember it.

It happened that Julia was the daughter of very wealthy parents—her father, Mr. Roswell-Smith, was president of Century Publications. Inness, a poor struggling artist, had just met her and had fallen deeply in love with her although he was very uncertain about her attitude toward him. It was all the more trying because there were few occasions to be with her at all.

At last opportunity arrived. He was invited to attend a big

dance at her home. He was beside himself with excitement. That evening, in his modest lodging, he put out all his finery—the black coat, starched shirt, silk tie, and his most treasured possession, the diamond studs made from his mother's earrings. He was standing there, gazing at them with happy anticipation, when he heard a knock at the door. It was a friend.

"George," the friend said, "I am in a terrible mess! I have to go to a party and the laundress did not bring my dress shirt. It is the only one I have and I beg you to lend me one of yours!"

Inness stared in dismay. "But I have only one myself, and as you see, I am also going to a party!"

"But, George, it is more than important for me to be there tonight. I am planning to propose to the girl I love and I have been waiting for this opportunity for months."

Inness thought of his own love for Julia and understood too well how his friend felt. After a minute of hesitation he told him he could have the shirt and then added, "And you can take the diamond studs too. But who is the girl?"

"Miss Roswell-Smith!" The friend left with such speed that he did not notice the expression of utter horror on George's face.

However, notwithstanding his elegant attire and the diamond studs, Miss Roswell-Smith did not respond to the eager admirer, and in a few weeks, as in any good story, George Inness and she were engaged to be married.

The Innesses' house, Cragsmoor, was enormous, without much style but commanding a fabulous outlook that stretched for miles around. Mr. Inness took us through rooms filled with paintings. At first I could not figure out which were his and which his famous father's, and later I learned what a tragedy this similarity of style was in his life. His father was so famous that it had been almost impossible for him to carve out his

own identity. To all the art dealers and the people who organized art shows he was not the "real" Inness. At one time he
was brought to such a state of despair that he took every
brush, paint, and canvas he had and burned them all up, determined never to paint again. Fortunately for him, he got over
that feeling, and at the time I knew him he was painting with
greatest abandon his green landscapes with rainy clouds dis-
solving in the hazy backgrounds which were so typical too of
his father.

After this visit, they came to call on us. Rising above the
rather shabby surroundings of our old farmhouse, they both
showed genuine interest in us and also in my brother's and my
paintings.

A few days later Mr. Inness appeared alone and to my utter
surprise asked me to paint a miniature of him. I am sure he
would not have done so if he did not like my work, but I also
think it was a spontaneous gesture of encouragement from an
accomplished artist to another who was just beginning a new
career under very unpredictable circumstances. I will always
be grateful to him for that and the manner in which it was
done.

Of course the portrait was to be for his beloved Julia, and to
be kept a deep secret from her. This secret from his wife was
the one thing that disturbed him and he mentioned it not once
but many times, saying that it was the first time he had
concealed anything from her.

The portrait was to be a profile on ivory. His profile was
exceptionally good but I regretted not being able to paint
his kind brown eyes. When it was completed, he expressed
satisfaction and to my consternation produced a check that
was double the prearranged amount. I was really overcome. As
I think of it now I still feel gratitude at having met somebody

like him. He not only strengthened my confidence in my work, he also gave me unwavering faith in the fine human side of my future subjects. His father might have been a greater artist but he could not have surpassed his son in those rare personal qualities that will always make George Inness, Jr., in my estimation, the real George Inness.

Soon after I had completed his portrait, Mr. Inness introduced us to an elderly gentleman by the name of Frank Seaman. He owned an estate a few miles away called Yama Farms, in Napanoch, New York. I will try to describe in a few words what sort of a place it was.

At that time, in the early twenties, Yama Farms was an institution that had no equal and I imagine never will. Frank Seaman was a big advertising man who started the whole thing by entertaining his friends at his country house in the mountains, the Hut, as he called it. As he was a very hospitable host, more and more of his friends wished to visit him. To provide space for them, he began building a rambling guest house to which more rooms were added; with the increase of visitors, as I understood by mutual decision, they became paying guests and Yama Farms was run as a business. The fees were high but the luxuries enjoyed had no equal. The best food and wines, a golf course, rooms with beautiful antique furniture, and all in a picturesque and completely isolated setting. Besides the most select company of guests—all the new ones had to be introduced by the original groups of friends—on weekends Mr. Seaman invited as his personal guests famous writers, explorers, men of science and art, renowned pianists, and outstanding men in all fields who were only too happy to visit this fabulous place and give talks or in some way share their talents.

The place ran up a large yearly deficit but Mr. Seaman, a man of great esthetic qualities and appreciative of all the fine things in life, had also a shrewd business sense and in entertaining his guests, he of course increased the accounts of his advertising firm. It was amazing how many representative of American business were sometimes gathered together at Yama Farms. If you were introduced to Mr. Waterman, it would be the fountain pen, Mr. Colgate, the soap, Mr. Eastman, the Kodak, and so on. The "famous four" who often visited Yama Farms during their camping trips together were Thomas Edison, Henry Ford, John Burroughs, and Harvey Firestone. All those people enjoyed the actual simplicity of life and the fact that no fuss was made over them. Above the fireplace in Mr. Seaman's "hut" were engraved the words of the great naturalist, John Burroughs: "It is so easy to get lost in this world. I come here to find myself." It was so true. They did come to find themselves, but they found others besides.

It was through this incredible place that we got our first real introduction to the United States. It was also here, in a completely natural and effortless way that my professional painting began and ever expanded. As a consequence of that visit, I was invited to stay for a few days to paint Mr. Seaman's portrait, and the visit turned out to be a great success. I discovered that more and more people were interested in my work. And that was the turning point.

Mr. Seaman persuaded us to sell our farm, which we did joyfully, and move to a house that he owned near Yama Farms. It was a lovely old building with white columns that reminded me of our house in Russia. My husband was, by that time, involved in a business enterprise in New York, and I settled down to painting, with ever increasing commissions. The house was within walking distance from Yama Farms and many guests came to visit us. There were still rather few Russians in the United States after the Revolution, and we were a sort of curiosity. I must say that the first pictures I did, except for a few of women and children, were of old gentlemen in gray suits and blue ties or brown suits and maroon ties, and were rather dull.

After five years of living near Yama Farms, we moved to Merrick, Long Island. My husband had become increasingly involved with Igor Sikorsky in his aeronautics firm, and I had become so well established as a painter that I knew my work would continue.

In 1928 my husband died in a swimming accident. Andrey had moved to Pittsburgh and my mother had passed away in 1933. I was on my own with three children (Elizabeth was born while we were living at Napanoch), my paint box, and complete faith that the good Lord would not leave me. I decided to move to Locust Valley, where I had a few friends.

In the years that followed, I received commissions from all over the United States, as well as Long Island. I was able to accept them thanks to the presence in our house of Tatassia, a gem of a person if there ever was one. I always had a cook, as I realized from the beginning that I could not afford to wash my own dishes. Tatassia (Alvina Schoening) was of German origin and had come from Russia with some distant relatives of ours. She took care of my mother when she was ill, and after her death, Tatassia stayed with us until she died in 1943.

I must admit that I never considered myself a professional artist. I had no real artistic training and always shunned publicity. But I had a God-given talent to capture the likeness of a person, especially the eyes. I always thought what a risk people took in asking a complete stranger to interpret the features and the spirit of those they loved. If I did not have the confidence that came from utter reliance on an inner Power and the knowledge of my technique, acquired through blunders and mistakes, I could have never ventured to accept those sometimes very complicated commissions.

In the chapters that follow, I offer my personal impressions of the subjects I painted and the circumstances surrounding the sittings. I have mentioned only what I have personally heard or seen as well as what was told to me directly, and just the highlights. It has certainly been a long career and the variety of my subjects, as well as the number, has been tremendous. I feel that through my paint box I have grasped a certain picture of many people generally well known but not always understood. I am not pretending to understand them myself but possibly to give another slant on their personalities.

CHAPTER TWO

Portraits from My Paint Box

RABINDRANATH TAGORE

One Christmas time, when we were still living near Yama Farms, my brother and I were privileged to paint a very remarkable person. The famous Hindu poet and philosopher, Rabindranath Tagore, was visiting Yama Farms. His handsome aristocratic appearance fascinated us all—those dark eyes, long white hair and beard, and flowing garments. He consented to pose for us one morning and arrived shortly after breakfast, walking down the snowy road from Yama Farms with Baron Rosen, who had been the Russian ambassador to the United States at the time of the humiliating 1905 Portsmouth Peace. Tagore was shown into the living room and Baron Rosen went to join my mother who was still drinking her coffee. Rosen was not amused with Tagore.

"I am really not responsible for bringing this Indian," he said, "I was walking down the hill to see you and he joined me."

Tagore looked like anything but an Indian. True, on the background of the dazzling morning snow he did appear a little odd, but with his high black hat and cape he more resembled a wandering Greek monk than anything else.

An armchair was placed in the middle of the room and

Rabindranath Tagore

Tagore was asked to sit while my brother and I, from different angles, began to work as rapidly as we could. Tagore posed magnificently in spite of the lively conversation that was carried on between him and my brother, which in no way interrupted the painting, but I am sorry that I hardly remember, in my concentration, what they were talking about. The only thing I do recall was Tagore's comparison of our present human existence with the unhatched chicken in the egg that pecks and pecks from within, not knowing what is awaiting him in the big world until the shell is finally broken and the real life begins.

Quite happy with the results of our labor, we asked Tagore to sign both pictures, which he did—in English and Hindustani. My brother gave his later to a friend, but I kept mine.

Before departing, Tagore put his hand in his pocket and took out a ten-cent piece. "Isn't it odd," he said in his perfect Oxford English, "that an old gentleman would give me this, while waiting for his car? Do I look like a tramp?"

That night we dined with Mr. Seaman and told him of the incident.

"Oh yes," was Mr. Seaman's casual remark, "that was John D. Rockefeller, Sr. He left several days ago, just as Tagore arrived."

How very strange that was! Here was a king of Eastern culture and a king of Western industry who met and never recognized each other!

JOHN BOWMAN

When my brother became director of the Carnegie Museum of Natural History in Pittsburgh in 1926, I visited him and was invited to many interesting dinners and parties. Commissions began pouring in; I believe that I painted more portraits in Pittsburgh than in any other city, mostly small watercolors. I had the opportunity to know many delightful and friendly people—and I think Pittsburgh was particularly full of them, contributing to the unusually warm and hospitable atmosphere that characterizes the city.

The first commission was Mrs. William Holland, the wife of the first director of the Carnegie Museum; this was followed by the Laughlins and, of course, the Joneses, of Jones & Laughlin Steel, a few of the Heinz 57 Varieties, the Aluminum Hunts, and a number of others.

Andrey Avinoff

For the museum, I painted Andrey in his academic gown, and his successor Dr. O. E. Jennings, who was responsible for giving my brother the idea of painting 250 watercolors of the wild flowers of Pennsylvania. Dr. Jennings helped to provide my brother with the flowers, and the paintings were later reproduced magnificently and published by the University of Pittsburgh Press under the supervision of Mrs. Agnes Starrett.

One portrait that I felt was indeed a privilege to paint was of Dr. John Bowman, chancellor of the University of Pittsburgh. He was a most outstanding man and contributed to the cultural life in Pittsburgh more than any other single individual. The remarkable Cathedral of Learning, which houses the university, is indeed a great institution. Towering with its Gothic grandeur of forty-two floors over the city, it was the complete creation of this man of vision and ideals. Dr. Bowman had a striking face that looked like some medieval monk; it lit up with inner fire and inspiration when he talked of his plans, past and future. His little book *The World That Was* (1926) is a touching and appealing story of himself as a little boy from four to six years old, with all his dreams and aspirations even then. His father used to read classical poetry to him and his older brother and, inspired by this, he felt that he wanted to be a poet. But somehow it was not the thing to do. To be a doctor, architect, scientist, and so on was all right, but a poet—oh no! He lived in the country and would go to his favorite spot back in the garden, the raspberry patch, and meditate there upon the hopelessness of his cherished dreams. He was then barely six years old but it seems that those ideals remained with him throughout his life. I certainly was aware, while painting him, of this inner drive to higher goals, untouched by the surrounding atmosphere of materialistic achievements, the business atmosphere of Pittsburgh.

The creation of the Cathedral of Learning was certainly the realization of his dreams. He told me that when he first came there as chancellor, the university quarters had little to offer. To make improvements, funds were needed. There were plenty of people in Pittsburgh who he knew could help but he did not want to ask. But that help did come, and he told me how he got his first million dollars. He asked for an appointment with Andrew Mellon, who agreed to see him but only with the understanding that there would be no soliciting of money. When he arrived Mr. Mellon greeted him cordially. Dr. Bowman's attention was drawn to a large painting by Rembrandt. "I read about it in the papers" he said. "You paid $500,000 for it." Dr. Bowman looked at the painting very attentively and asked, "How much do you think the actual material for this picture is worth?"

Mr. Mellon looked a little puzzled. He replied, "Well, maybe twenty-five dollars."

"Then for what did you pay $499,975?"

Silence.

"You paid that sum for the genius of Rembrandt."

Mr. Mellon agreed.

"Then, Mr. Mellon, you will understand what I am trying to do. There are plenty of geniuses in the university and I am trying to help in bringing out those abilities of the boys and girls who come here by bus from the steel mills and mining towns of the suburbs of Pittsburgh."

Mr. Mellon caught what he was aiming at. "I see what you mean. I will have my secretary write you a check for $500,000."

"That is not enough," Dr. Bowman said, "because my cause is worth much more than the genius of a dead man."

Mr. Mellon called his secretary, inquired about the balance

John G. Bowman

in some of his banks, and then wrote a check for one million dollars!

THE MELLONS

During my first years of painting in Pittsburgh I inevitably met the Mellon family. My first Mellon portrait was of little Cordelia, age five, daughter of Sarah M. Scaife, Richard Mellon's sister. While I was painting that picture Mrs. Scaife asked me not to use it for publicity. Little did she know how I dreaded it myself! Later I painted a small watercolor of her husband Alan Scaife in a scarlet coat; her son Richard, nine, then a rather naughty but entertaining little boy; and again Cordelia as a debutante. The family of William Larimer Mellon passed through my brush without any particular excitement. It was the Richard King Mellons who have kept me busy with many portraits.

As usual it started with the children. During World War II, Colonel Mellon, whom I will call Dick from now on, and his wife Connie were living in Washington with their four adopted children. I stayed with them several times while I was painting there; even when I did the first portrait of FDR in 1943 (the Mellons were hardly admirers of Roosevelt, but they were quite interested in my reports about my White House encounters).

I had a good time talking with Dick. Later, in the relaxed atmosphere of their house at Woods Hole on Cape Cod, I painted him in his colonel's uniform. The portrait was a small watercolor with Dick leaning both arms on a table and part of his cap showing on one side. We joked that a Martini or Scotch highball was missing on the other side of the portrait. I had used the same composition with the cap for a portrait of

Richard K. Mellon

my son in his navy uniform, following the suggestion of his wife, and it worked very well.

Dick was wearing all kinds of decorations on his colonel's uniform, and one was particularly complicated. My brother, who excelled in making the most intricate details in his paintings, did them for me. A few years later I received a letter from Dick asking if I could not change something in the uniform on the portrait as he had been promoted to general. I said I was sure I could. Then he had an afterthought. "The portrait is still a good likeness," he wrote, "so I believe I would rather have a second identical one in the general's uniform. I think I still look like you painted me then." So the portrait arrived and I got to work on the replica, but my one problem was the famous decoration. My brother had died, and I had the time of my life duplicating it.

Shortly after the painting was finished, I was notified that Dick and his wife would be in New York on their way to Europe and would stop at my apartment to see it. When they arrived I looked at Dick. His face was much older looking— his hair was grayer, he had bags under his eyes. Connie took one glance at the two portraits. "Who is that young man?" she laughed. So I took up my brushes and paints and Dick was aged ten years within one hour!

I came to know this remarkable family very well. For Chatham College in Pittsburgh, which she supported, I did a portrait of Dick's mother, Jennie King Mellon, from the only photograph they had of her as a young girl, and I painted other members of the family up to the fourth generation. One thing that particularly struck me was the training they received as children. Connie told me how Dick's mother, and later Dick himself, impressed upon all the children the responsibility of having such a fortune. They had to redeem the fact that they were so rich by sharing their wealth privately in their early years and later, when they came of age, by distributing it through foundations that each had to control. I am sure that little has ever been known about this by the general public.

THE HUNTS

If Chancellor Bowman was the most outstanding man I painted in Pittsburgh, I would certainly consider Mrs. Rachel McMaster Miller Hunt the most remarkable and cultured woman who ever appeared in that city. Mrs. Hunt was unusually tiny, but in that diminutive body was stored so much energy, knowledge, curiosity, and practical ability that even she jokingly called herself "the mighty midget." Her principal interest was books, including book-binding, and prints, mainly botanical. On the top floor of the beautiful house on Ellsworth Avenue where she lived with her family was an authentic reproduction of a medieval book-binding studio. All the equipment was antique but it was there not just for display, like a museum rarity, but was used by her to make the finest artistic bindings you could imagine, of rare leathers with intricate gilded designs, often embellished with semiprecious stones. The collection of books that she had bound herself was a superb achievement. Her library was magnificent, with bookshelves up to the high ceiling and a gallery around the top. In this beautiful room her distinguished guests gathered to converse after dinner. Being interested in anything connected with botany, Rachel naturally participated in all the American Garden Club activities, giving lectures everywhere. Her greatest achievement later was the creation, together with her husband Roy, of the remarkable Hunt Botanical Library, in the penthouse of Hunt Library at Carnegie Mellon Univer-

Rachel McMasters Miller Hunt

sity. Like the Frick Collection, the penthouse was a gem in itself. The library houses all her rare books, with rare pieces of furniture. Roy, being the big cheese of aluminum, had made practically the whole building of that metal. But when it came to Rachel's library, she said, "Now, Roy, I don't want any of the aluminum here!"

Roy was a quiet, reserved man, quite a contrast to his wife except for also being rather short in stature. Always interested in the family histories of the people I painted, I enjoyed talking to them both about theirs. Roy told me how his father and another friend started Alcoa. I had always wondered why they used the word *aluminum* instead of *aluminium*, as it was spelled in Canada. Roy said that when his father and partner started the business, practically from scratch, they settled in very modest headquarters. It was to be called the Aluminium Corporation of America. They had ordered the business blocks for stationery and so forth, but unfortunately, the engraver made a mistake by dropping the second letter. *i*, which made it *aluminum* instead of *aluminium*. As they could not afford to do the whole thing over, they decided to keep it that way—and besides it somehow sounded better.

I never painted Roy's portrait, but I did a watercolor of Rachel with an old tapestry in the background done by my brother. I also painted many portraits later of their children and grandchildren.

THE FRICKS

Shortly before Christmas one year I was painting a small watercolor of the son of Miss Helen Clay Frick's lawyer, William Moorehead, in his home in Pittsburgh. As I looked at the dreary winter scene from the window with light snow coming down, I saw a rather slight, nondescript woman coming to the entrance. Her general appearance reminded me of some social worker who might be collecting funds for Christmas charities. Mrs. Moorehead introduced her as Miss Frick and I was a little startled to say the least. For the next ten years I did not see her again.

In the meantime, while living in Locust Valley, I met her brother Childs and his family. He and my brother, who was then director of the Carnegie Museum in Pittsburgh, had become very good friends as a result of their mutual interest in natural science. That particular interest was, as I understand it, the cause of the friction that grew between Childs and his father, Henry Clay Frick, who was disappointed to see his son drifting away from the coal and steel industry.

Childs and his family lived in Roslyn, Long Island. He had a beautiful estate on the top of a hill. The house was built in the midst of a park designed by the great landscape wizard, Umberto Innocenti, with acres and acres of different varieties of trees. The most attractive part of it was a beautiful garden with very special flowering bushes, decorative trees, roses, and flowers which Innocenti and Mrs. Frick (who was a gardening expert herself) had created together. The house was quite grandiose, typical of those big mansions on Long Island that grew like mushrooms in the twenties, built by different tycoons who made their fortunes elsewhere and came to spend them here. It was the first time, in the United States, that I was in such an impressive house. It was full of beautiful things, and lots of flowers. My brother, who had come to visit me in Locust Valley, was invited for dinner by the Fricks and I was included too. The house had some sort of arcade on both sides looking out into the gardens and it was there that we had cocktails.

Mrs. Frick was a lovely woman with dark hair and brown eyes. She wore a very becoming light gray chiffon dress. Mr. Frick was a tall man, bald and grayish, wearing a pince-nez, with blue eyes and a high-pitched voice. He had a delightfully wry sense of humor. You never knew if he was serious or joking. While we were sipping martinis from shallow silver cups, two of the children appeared, a son Clay, at that time a rather stout youngster, and Martha, one of their three daughters, a striking brunette not unlike her mother. Of course all of them had their portraits painted, up to the fourth generation (or the fifth, if you include the posthumous portraits of Henry Clay Frick, Sr., and his wife). I started with Mrs. Frick, a medium-size oval watercolor. She wore the same gray chiffon dress she had worn that first night, and held a long-haired dachshund on her lap. (I think there were at least a half dozen of these dogs in the house; they even had their own little private exits in some rooms.) We put the garden with part of the lake showing from afar in the background of the portrait. During the sittings, I came to know Mrs. Frick quite well. Besides her skill in gardening, she was very knowledgeable about birds and could identify the chirping of each one as it came from the open windows.

There was something quite sad about Mrs. Frick's face when she was in repose, but in conversation she was very amusing and had an extremely sharp tongue. The wistful expression that I could not escape putting in her eyes had rather obvious cause. Mr. Frick, who adored her, would never let her out of his sight. He would not allow her to ride a horse because a friend of hers was killed during a hunt. She was living a very isolated life in a gilded cage.

I continued to paint the Frick family—Childs Frick and the children as they got married and produced their children.

They were all rather small watercolors. At one time Mr. Frick mentioned that he thought there should be a portrait of his sister for the Frick Collection in New York. That's how it came about that I myself later felt that she should be represented. She was a perfect subject for a small watercolor portrait, with her pale blue eyes, grayish hair, and pale complexion, but, as we discovered, she was adamant about not having it done.

In the late forties Mr. Frick asked me to do a life-size portrait of his father for the Duquesne Club in Pittsburgh, It was to be in watercolor, as I did not do many oils then, and had to be based on photographs. (Henry Clay Frick died in 1919). I learned that Miss Frick was not very enthusiastic about the idea and refused to give any photographs for the project. But there was one very good one and I started anyway. When I had more or less completed the head, leaving the rest unfinished, my brother urged me to show it to Mr. Frick in that stage. "You will ruin it if you go on," he said. And I knew, of course, of my ability to do that! So I showed it to Mr. Frick and he agreed that it was good in its present stage. But he still wanted another one, for the Duquesne Club, keeping the first painting for himself.

"I think my sister should see it," he said. "I will call her up."

I was actually on my way to visit my son's family in Bedford, New York, and Miss Frick's place was close by. She agreed to see the painting, rather under pressure, as I understood. Mrs. Frick made a rather sarcastic remark about not envying me showing the portrait to her sister-in-law. Anyway, I departed. I had never been at her home before. It was an old farmhouse in a lovely rural setting with a dirt road leading to the entrance. The rooms were dark, with low ceilings, anything but spacious. Such a contrast with the Frick mansion in Roslyn! Miss Frick greeted me with cool courtesy. I showed her the portrait. She looked at it for a while in silence.

"I think of all the portraits that have been done of my father," she finally said, "this is the best likeness. Could you do one identical replica for me?" I was so startled I don't know what I mumbled. Later I began to think what a challenge it was going to be to copy the rather casual strokes of the watercolor, but I started on it right away. It came out very close, but I could see a slight difference in expression. It was rather softer than the first. My old maid, Marie, who always came to inspect my portraits, was particularly impressed.

"Quelle douce figure," she said. "He looks so gentle."

I am sure I had not invented it. In the photograph that I used as a model, Mr. Frick looked more like the rather tough businessman that most people saw, but I am sure there was a very different side to him which was expressed in his devotion to his daughter and appreciation of creation in art. When Miss Frick saw the finished painting, she surprised me by saying that she liked this one much better than the first. The only thing she fussed about was the shape of his ear.

"It is like a shell," she said.

It took some time to please her because the photo did not show it very clearly. When everything finally was accomplished, she gave me a check that was double the amount I asked, just like Mr. Inness so many, many years ago. This portrait was used for the magnificent illustrated catalogue of the paintings in the Frick Collection and later hung in her penthouse over the adjacent Library for Art Research.

This was the beginning of a wonderful friendship. I know that as far as she was concerned, the fact that I rendered a likeness of her father to her complete satisfaction played a main part. I became truly devoted to her. I did not always agree with some of her ideas about art and politics, but I saw in her an extremely loyal and idealistic, shy and lovable person on one side and an extremely intolerant, belligerent and difficult-to-approach person on the other. Having been a frequent visitor to Pittsburgh for years, I was invited to stay at her house there, which I did several times. Clayton, on Penn Avenue in the neighborhood known as Homewood, was the old residence of her parents before they moved to New York. Helen had preserved all its details exactly as they were when they all lived there. It was another antique specimen of a late-nineteenth century home of a wealthy family, with lots of mahogany, damask, oriental rugs, beautiful china and crystal, fine linens, dim lamps, and old-fashioned bath fixtures. I was curious to know how it happened that the exquisite Frick house in New York, where the art collection is now, was built in such contrast to the Pittsburgh residence. Helen told me that it began with a trip to Europe that Mr. Frick made as a young man, together with his friend, Andrew Mellon. When they were in London, Mr. Frick was very much impressed by the Wallace Collection and said that he hoped some day to create something similar in the United States. In time, he built the beautiful house on Fifth Avenue. Elsie de Wolf did the decorating (it was her first job, and with unlimited funds) and Umberto Innocenti did the planting. When the magnolias are in bloom, I always think of him.

After Mr. Frick died, his widow, with Helen, lived in the house a few years longer; when she passed away, the dream of a young man became a reality. The Frick Collection is so far superior to the Wallace and is such a gem by itself, that I truly believe that nowhere in this world is there anything so perfect. All credit goes to Mr. Frick, who showed great appreciation of art and was attentive to good advice, and to Helen, whose final touches brought his dream to realization. I was honored when she asked me to do a small portrait of her mother for the Collection. She said that visitors saw the portrait of her father and often asked if there was a Mrs. Frick. Fortunately she had a very good picture of her mother when she was quite young, in a very attractive pose. I eliminated the dark background and did a small oval picture in the Peter Sokoloff style. It was placed on a round table in the Boucher room, and there are always fresh roses next to it. I feel privileged to have even a small painting in this special place, though I fully realize that it is there not for its artistic merit but because of the subject.

When she later, for various reasons, ended her official connection with the Frick Collection, Helen continued with other projects. As might be expected, they had to do with the memory of her father. I am not sure if I heard it from her or somebody very close to her, but apparently she was disturbed by the criticism that although he had made his fortune in Pittsburgh, he moved to New York and arranged to have the Frick Collection presented to that city. So she decided that she should do something similar in his memory for Pittsburgh. Before any plans were seriously considered, she acquired the famous collection of copies of Florentine paintings by Nicolas Lokhoff and presented them as a gift to the University of Pittsburgh. A lot of people were not enthusiastic.

"Why copies and not originals?" they asked.

People did not know that these were not just ordinary copies. In fact I think it was a very interesting story. It was told to me by an Italian friend who knew Lokhoff. In the early part of the century, shortly before World War I, the Russian emperor got carried away by the idea that it would be wonderful to have perfect copies of the best of the Italian Renaissance paintings for the Russian people to see, particularly for those who would never be able to go to Italy to see the originals. Lokhoff was a professor at the Academy of Art in St. Petersburg, and though not a great creative artist, he knew all the tricks of the old masters' techniques and could make excellent copies. So he was commissioned to make the closest possible reproductions of about twenty of the best specimens of art in Florence. After he established himself there, he spent about two years thoroughly studying the old masters' secrets, including the tools, and techniques that were used for gilding parts of paintings. And then he started his work. It took many years to complete, and in his utter concentration, he hardly noticed world events—the war, the European upheaval. When the work was done, the tsar was dead and old Russia was gone. As he held an official commission from the Russian government, he contacted the Soviets. No response; they had nothing to do with it. And there he was with all these paintings that nobody wanted. He did not live too long after that and I am sure he died of a broken heart. The collection survived World War II intact, and in the middle fifties Bernard Berenson, who knew Lokhoff and had seen the marvelous work he had done, gave Helen the idea to acquire the paintings for some of her future projects (one or two paintings were acquired by the Fogg Museum).

The official presentation of this collection was in the very impressive Commons Room in the Cathedral of Learning at the University of Pittsburgh. It was a magnificent affair. The paintings were hung all around that grandiose room. Contemporary music was played on the instruments depicted in his paintings, which, by themselves, were really superb. Some, in my opinion, were quite unbelievably identical to the originals. Later, Helen constructed at the university a building similar to the Frick Collection with loggias around a little garden

Helen Clay Frick

created by Innocenti. It had a real Italian atmosphere. The Lokhoff copies were hung around the garden in the loggias. After some unfortunate misunderstandings with the university, Helen later built another very beautiful museum (the Frick Art Museum) on the premises of the Old Frick residence in Homewood.

Thanks to this new museum, my wish was finally realized and I did paint Helen's portrait. In the museum there is a room that replicates her father's study in his house at Pride's Crossing, Massachusetts. Through the window you can see a panorama of the garden. There are no particular paintings, mostly photographs. When I was there it occurred to me that it was a good place to have a small portrait of Helen, who personally created this museum. Virginia Lewis, the director, agreed with me.

I knew I could not hope for any sittings from Helen, but as I had painted her mother from much earlier photographs, I thought I might do the same with her. So I began asking members of her family if they had any photographs—and one was found, just after World War II for the English girls she sheltered during those years.

I began studying her face, her coloring, and finally a very light, small watercolor emerged. I knew how angry she would be, but I took the risk and presented it to her as a Christmas gift. She wrote me a very sweet letter with a mild reprimand, but said something that really made me laugh. "You made me look like a lady."

A few years later during a visit I had with her in Bedford, she brought up the subject of the portrait. She said she really could not accept it and had to give me a check. I violently protested saying that there are times when you have to be able to accept gifts graciously. In a few days, however, I received a very substantial check. Again I remembered dear Mr. George Inness who so many, many years ago, in those first difficult years of my artistic career, gave me a feeling that I might meet more people like him whose generosity really went beyond expectation.

Helen had great energy and a unique ability to create settings for beautiful things. Many times I have attended private receptions at the former Frick residence in New York. I don't know when I have been present at anything quite so elegant — all the rooms lighted, the wonderful paintings, the flowers, the distinguished crowd, the beautiful music. If you have not seen it, it is difficult to describe, but "a thing of beauty is a joy forever," and that is how I feel when I think of it.

THE DU PONTS

In the middle thirties, after painting several members of the polo-playing group in Westbury, I received a commission from one of them. J. P. Mills, a perfectly charming, strikingly handsome young man, asked me to paint his wife Alice, the daughter of Felix du Pont. She was a lovely blonde with dark eyes, gay, enthusiastic, interested in everything under the sun. After thirty years we continued to be the best of friends. I painted her on Long Island at her in-laws' house in Glen Cove, and when I finished, her mother appeared unexpectedly from Wilmington. It is not easy to describe Mrs. Felix du Pont, or Dick, as everybody called her. I became quite devoted to her in spite of many traits that could not be condoned and of which she was totally unaware. She was so pleased with her daughter's likeness that she invited me to Wilmington to do all of her children. I joyfully landed in the midst of that remarkable family, whose members I am still painting to this day.

Dick and her family lived in a big rambling house, surrounded by gardens with beautiful flowers. The house was
filled with them, also with antiques, but nothing really showed
to advantage because everything was so cluttered up. I noticed
that it gave a great opportunity for Dick to rearrange the
furniture from time to time or to replace it with other items.
Her husband was a quiet retiring man, extremely cultured,
and I saw how these activities irritated him. I hardly knew him
because shortly after we met them he faded out of the picture
and they got a divorce.

Dick was of a rather heavy build with a weather-beaten face,
not handsome at all, but quite patrician. Her hair was messy,
her clothes rather gaudy, of many colors, and she wore lots of
beads and gold for evening events. Her hats, masses of them,
were fantastic, with feathers of all types, and she wore them at
all angles. She was a great sportswoman and a magnificent
shot. Shooting wild turkey or quail on her South Carolina
plantation was one of her favorite pastimes. But I believe
she most loved flowers. Her knowledge and love of them was,
like many other du Ponts, particularly strong. Hunting for antiques was another occupation that I had the opportunity to
enjoy while driving with her in the country.

One evening I saw one of her night-blooming cereus
blossoms and said how I wished my brother and I could paint
it. Believe it or not, shortly thereafter, she called me up at my
Long Island home and said she was sending one that was
about to blossom, in a station wagon straight to Locust Valley.
I was particularly happy because it just happened that my
brother was there from Pittsburgh and he was especially adept
at flower painting. We placed the plant, which had several
buds, on our terrace, and when darkness settled, the beautiful
lilylike flowers opened up, filling the air with sweet heavy

perfume. Such excitement! We were all prepared with flood lights and paints and started feverishly on our work, my brother, my daughter Zoric, and myself. I am afraid the results of that night of painting were far from the exquisite beauty of the original, but it left a memory of a fabulous night and a wonderful gesture by a great lady from Wilmington. It was fortunate that she had so many different interests because her life was not too happy. She was crushed by her divorce and lost a daughter and a son through accidents. However, in her middle sixties, she married a glamour-boy about her own age and lived happily until the day she died.

After I had painted most of her family, I found myself engaged with more of the du Ponts. The one that I somehow came to know better than the others was Mrs. Irénée du Pont. She was Felix du Pont's sister-in-law and, like him, was very retiring and almost shy. She spoke so softly she could hardly be heard. Like so many of her family, she had dark eyes and must have been very good looking as a younger woman. I painted five of her eight daughters and three of their husbands. Her own picture was actually done from an old photograph that she liked, but she posed for the coloring.

While I was painting I stayed with them at Granogue, an enormous house on the top of a hill with a beautiful view all around. The rooms were spacious, filled with flowers and all kinds of interesting pictures, sculpture, and whatnot. A whole wing of the house was a regular museum with samples of rocks and precious stones artificially illuminated in all colors. It was all so cozy and friendly that I felt completely at my ease staying there. Mr. Irénée du Pont was a delightful man with a twinkle in his eyes, a particular favorite with all the girls; I did not really see much of him but when I did, he was most interesting to talk to. The only time he really was rather somber was when talking of the political situation. It was in 1937–1938 and he was not happy about the Roosevelt administration and what it was doing to the economy of the country. I got along beautifully with his wife. I had always believed in health foods, which I am sure are partly responsible for my good health, and so was she, together with her companion Miss Frost. The latter was an old friend of hers, a rather plain typical little spinster with gray hair, frail looking, but very forceful nevertheless. She helped to raise the eight daughters and son, and continued to live at Granogue. Everyone called her Aunt Rebee. All three of us, particularly during those health food luncheons, discussed health foods and metaphysical literature. I have noticed that those two items generally appear together and their advocates are listed as crackpots!

One of Mrs. du Pont's great interests was old-time music and old instruments. She once invited me to a concert in New York given by a company which I am sure she helped financially. It was like being in the eighteenth century or even earlier. I am afraid I was not too appreciative. During one of my visits, she took me to visit N. C. Wyeth who was a great friend of theirs and lived not too far away. He was rather startling looking, with very bushy hair; you felt you were in the presence of a great individual. I had always admired his classic illustrations but never had seen his paintings. We were there late at night. He took us to his studio and I was most impressed by a mural he had just finished. It depicted a dream he once had: George Washington, mounted on a horse, was surrounded by lots of people, and in the front was Mr. Wyeth himself in a long nightgown looking at the procession. I was so grateful to have had the privilege to visit this remarkable artist. I understand what an influence he must have had on his son Andrew, whose outstanding talent is now so admired and appreciated.

I did not see any particular interest in great paintings among the du Pont family. They had no great collection of works of old or modern artists. Interest in gardens and flowers predominated and, of course, American antiques. I doubt if anything could surpass the famous du Pont estate Winterthur in this particular category.

The home of Harry (Henry Francis) du Pont in Southampton, although less well known, was also a gem. A funny incident happened while I stayed there painting his two daughters. As I was starting on one of the portraits, I threw a sheet over a screen for a background. The screen was near the fireplace and as I threw the sheet, I managed to hit a little chalk squirrel holding an apple that was on the mantelpiece, and it fell on the floor, breaking in several pieces. I was so distressed, knowing how Harry prized everything he had in the house, that I collected the pieces and asked Mrs. du Pont not to tell him. The next time I returned I brought the squirrel, repaired to perfection, and presented it to him. Harry could not understand what it was all about and said something to the effect that I should not have bothered. At that moment I noticed a triangular hutch in the corner of the room with twenty identical squirrels!

Mrs. Harry du Pont was not interested, I believe, in all those antiques. Playing bridge is what she liked, and it was her husband who took particular interest in table arrangements and flowers. I was told that every morning he gave instructions as to what linen, china, and flower arrangements were to be used for luncheons and dinners. Funnily enough, I clearly remember only one setting, a luncheon. The tablecloth was turquoise linen and there was a bowl of sunflowers in the

middle; all the rest was pewter—plates, tumblers, and finger
bowls. Everything was fine until the vanilla ice cream was
served. Somehow it did not look right on a pewter plate. I am
sure an apple pie would have been better.

Harry du Pont's knowledge and impeccable taste in everything was particularly obvious when he participated in the
refurbishing of the White House during the Kennedy years. I
understand he was responsible in great part for the beauty of
the guest rooms. Several years later, when I had the opportunity of staying in one of those rooms, I was really impressed
with the beauty and harmony of the surroundings. However,
not all members of the du Pont family accomplished anything
so spectacular. Their houses were very beautiful, with lots of
flowers, but they were, first of all, cozy, and somehow I was
never too conscious of the furnishings.

Before closing my impressions of that family, I must mention Crawford Greenewalt. He was, at the time I painted him,
the president of the company. His wife was a daughter of the
Irénée du Ponts, very beautiful and brilliant, and he was the
nephew of Mrs. W. K. du Pont, who was Lebanese, like her
sister, Greenewalt's mother. I think he was the most brilliant of
all the men and had tremendous charm. He occupied the most
responsible post on account of his abilities; the du Ponts did
not put any family member in a responsible position unless he
deserved it. Crawford most certainly did. Photography was his
main hobby, particularly color photography. Later he was responsible for a magnificent publication on humming birds.

At the time I met Greenewalt, 1939, there was a great de-
velopment in the du Pont industries: lucite and nylon were
just appearing on the horizon. One day he presented me with
a pair of apricot-colored stockings. It was a first sample of
what later would be worn by every woman. He told me a very

sad story connected with it. It seemed they had a remarkable man in the company by the name of Wallace Carothers who had worked for years before developing from water, coal, and air, a product that was the foundation of what later was called nylon. He was overworked and terribly depressed, particularly by the fact that he could never do anything as spectacular in the future. So one day he committed suicide.

Lucite interested me because it was like glass yet not quite so shiny. I was always aware of the reflection on the glass covering my watercolor portraits. We discussed that matter with Crawford, particularly in connection with a painting owned by his aunt, Mrs. W. K. du Pont, a portrait of Anna Pavlova as the Dying Swan by a Russian artist, S. Sorin. It was very large and the background was black, so all you saw was your own reflection. We discussed the possibilities of producing a nonreflecting surface which would solve many problems both here and in museums where glass is required (an idea that was later realized).

THE WOODRUFFS

It always amazed me, as my career progressed, how a seemingly insignificant, almost casual, encounter developed into extremely interesting activities. I had become well established in Wilmington, painting members of the du Pont family, when a meeting of that type occurred. I had done a portrait of Mina Ross, whose mother, Mrs. W. K. du Pont, was Lebanese; and her daughter had inherited her oriental looks and was stunningly beautiful. I then went to work on one of her husband, Don Ross, whom I painted in a standing position holding a stopwatch with the Delaware racetrack in the background. As I was finishing the portrait, a quite handsome, debonair man dropped in together with an extremely beautiful woman. They were introduced as Mr. and Mrs. Woodruff, which meant nothing to me at the time. I will call them Bob and Nell from now on.

Bob came to look at what I was doing and made a rather fresh remark which, naturally, did not endear him to me. They left very shortly after and I did not see them for quite a while. Later that year I was approached by Nell with a request to paint her portrait. When I met her again at her house, which was quite modern compared to the mansions of the du Ponts, she told me that she was anxious to give her husband a small watercolor of herself as a present for their silver wedding anniversary. She looked so young and pretty, I could hardly believe she had been married so long. She warned me that it would be very difficult to please Bob as he had discarded all her previous pictures. Regardless, I felt no qualms about it. She particularly wanted one of the old-fashioned ovals which were a speciality of mine. The portrait turned out to be a great success, and I was overjoyed by the telegram she sent me from Hot Springs where they celebrated their anniversary.

After that she contacted me about painting Bob's portrait. Knowing that he would never sit for it, she made a point to invite me to their Georgia plantation and catch him there unprepared. By that time I had discovered that Bob was chairman of the board of the Coca-Cola Company, and their real residence was in Atlanta. In the fall of 1938 I arrived there to stay with them for a few days before going to the plantation. My first impression of that romantic city was enhanced by the preparations for the *Gone With the Wind* pageant. The spirit of that period impressed me so deeply that later, when I painted women in Atlanta, I always had them wear something of that era, never sweaters or sports clothes.

Robert W. Woodruff

Ichoway, the Woodruff's plantation, was a spacious yet cozy house with that particular smell of firewood mixed with the delicious odor of Southern food. Everything was made for having a good time, which I certainly had, in a special way, but the rest was a headache. After Bob got over the first shock and finally condescended to be painted, he made things very difficult for my work. He had many friends staying there and they were present most of the time; I did not particularly like this, but when we were alone he was bored. I did not know him well enough to make conversation and besides, he had a way of making me irritated. I even told him that I refused to get mad at him, which seemed to cheer him up. He was also pleased that I dipped my brush occasionally into a glass of Coca-Cola instead of water. I told him that I hoped the mysterious ingredients that were put in Coca-Cola would not affect the painting! Fortunately, it has survived unchanged, and he liked it better than the next four pictures I did of him.

What was very unusual about my painting connection with Bob was that besides doing many of his relatives (he and Nell had no children) he asked me to do portraits of several of his friends and associates, which he gave as presents. I painted his lawyer, his banker, his advertising manager, and his senator, Walter George of Georgia. Senator George was an impressive example of a real statesman, very kindly and easy to talk to. I painted him in the Senate building, in his office, sitting in a mahogany armchair by his desk. Though it was a small water-color, it took me some months to finish because we could never get together on dates. Finally Bob got mad. At our last sitting, I had a miserable cold and the senator was glum and distracted because something very unpleasant was going on between him and Henry Wallace. But we both kept the appointment. I called up Bob in Atlanta and announced that the portrait was finished.

"I suppose from now on you will not talk to me," I said.

"Oh no," he answered, "I want to talk to you about three more portraits."

In fact, there were a lot more commissions from Bob. One day we counted them and there were twelve. So he said, "Let's have two more!" I wonder how so many people really knew what a kind, thoughtful, and generous person he was. He usually acted like an oriental potentate, a sort of dictator, rather arrogant, particularly with his business associates. Then suddenly, his real nature would come out—sweet, gentle, almost sentimental. I became particularly fond of Nell, who had been his guardian angel all their life together. I am sure that with her inspiration they did much good and contributed so much more to philanthropy than is really known. When Nell died very suddenly, he asked me to do a portrait of her, on the basis of recent snaps, for the nursing home that was to be built in her name. I had very little to go by, just my memory and those very poor photographs. I believe it was really an inspired portrait because a former president of the home wrote me a letter saying that when the picture was unveiled, it was like a light in the room. Here, certainly, was an example of how a successful businessman and his wife shared their wealth with hundreds less fortunate than they and in a way that was often concealed.

MRS. DOUD

I remember the early 1950s, after the election of President Eisenhower, as a very gay and happy time. There was a specially joyful atmosphere all over the country and I personally recall it as particularly easy and pleasant.

Bob Woodruff, who was a good friend of Ike's, asked me to paint a watercolor portrait of Mrs. Eisenhower's mother, Mrs.

Elivera Doud, as a present to her daughter. Of course, I was enchanted. It was arranged that Nell and I would fly to Washington in the Coca-Cola plane. I had not been to the White House since FDR's time, and I felt a little self-conscious about being there again. All I had in mind was *not* to meet the president of the United States!

I found Mrs. Doud a delightful old lady, full of fun, unassuming, and completely at ease in that rather formal atmosphere. She expressed the desire to be painted in the dress she wore for the Inaugural Ball. I was a little dismayed by her choice. It was an ultramarine blue gown which was most unpaintable for the small oval portrait I was supposed to do of her. Besides, she had a blue costume-jewelry necklace that made it even worse. Unfortunately there was no way out. We established ourselves on the third floor which, at the time, was not as elegant as it is now.

"It is not easy to readjust to all of these new surroundings," Mrs. Doud said. "You can't even go in an elevator without being escorted." She said she missed the rural atmosphere of her home in Colorado, but she felt her presence was a great help to the president and her daughter and I certainly understood what she meant. She was so easy-going that you felt completely comfortable and happy with her. I am sure she was the same person in the White House as she was sitting in a rocking chair on the porch of her Colorado home. She said she played the guitar and I wish I could have heard her play. We discussed many subjects, particularly religious and spiritual literature, in which we had a mutual interest. We really got along beautifully.

I did not meet Mrs. Eisenhower right away as her days were crowded with different commitments. Mrs. Doud told me that one day Mrs. Eisenhower had received seventy-five nuns and had developed a frightful headache from the strain. When I was finally introduced to her, she was in bed, in a pink satin bed jacket, resting, I suppose, after a similar ordeal. When I was there a second time, I saw her again rather fleetingly, and also her sister, Mrs. Moore, who was a great help with the painting.

Mrs. Eisenhower was rather noncommital about her mother's portrait, and I don't blame her because I really thought the blue dress ruined it. The only pleasing remark I had, as I was told, was from the president, whom I had not met. When informed that my portrait was in watercolor he just said "Gee whiz!" He himself was finding relaxation in painting in oils under the guidance of the English artist Stevens, whose portrait of him now hangs in the White House. On that, my connection with the Eisenhowers ended, and I felt it was the fault of the blue lace dress.

THE ROYAL FAMILY OF LUXEMBOURG

In addition to traveling throughout the United States, I had the good fortune to paint many portraits in Great Britain and Europe. In London I painted the grandson of Otto Kahn; the daughter of Lady Lewison Gower; the Marquess of Milford Haven, who was best man at the wedding of the future Queen Elizabeth; and the chaplain of the archbishop of Canterbury— in his coronation robes, holding the Canterbury cross.

One outstanding trip took me to Luxembourg in the summer of 1974 at the invitation of Joan Dillon, the wife of Prince Charles of Luxembourg, who wanted me to paint her two children.

After a most formal correspondence, all the details were worked out. In the beginning of May I landed in Luxembourg with my granddaughter Victoria, practically in the arms of Major Prussen, the aide-de-camp of the Grand Duchess Charlotte, who was waiting for us at the end of the airplane ladder. His car was close by—no customs, passports, or anything. Everything was a red carpet. Major Prussen himself was somebody that you could not describe in words; you had to meet him. He had the manners of an eighteenth-century courtier, very formal but warm and charming. His whole face, with shining blue eyes, expressed cordiality and eagerness to be of assistance, which was given in every way throughout our whole visit. We were put up at the Grand Hotel Cravat, and all my requests for painting conditions were fulfilled. A room with a north light was turned into a regular studio, and beautiful flowers were supplied by Prince Charles and Joan. There was a memo from Major Prussen with a schedule of the hours when the children would be available to pose, many more memos followed as we progressed in our Luxembourg activities.

I must say that my subjects were adorable. The little girl, Charlotte, aged six, wore her hair in pigtails; Robert, five, in a white blouse and an old-fashioned jabot, was the picture of a little European prince, with blue eyes and a mop of golden wavy hair.

Charlotte listened attentively to all my stories, particularly the one about the frog princess, and my Blue Rabbit who lived down, down, down in the rabbit hole and had three little sisters, Fluffy, Muffy, and Tuffy. She thought instead of Tuffy, it would be more appropriate to call her Puffy! They were the most beautifully behaved children and their elderly nurse, Justine, kept them immaculately neat and tidy. The portraits turned out to everyone's satisfaction and the next thing I knew I was asked to paint their parents at some later

*The daughter and son
of Prince Charles
of Luxembourg*

Charlotte

Robert

date. I was pleased because I really felt very happy in that tiny little country.

Before I left I had the perfectly delightful experience of having luncheon with the grandmother, the Grand Duchess Charlotte, who lived in a beautiful country house called Fischbach. I was driven there, with Victoria and my other granddaughter, Antonia, who had joined us.

The grand duchess was the epitome of a true great lady, "la grande dame de l'Europe," as I mentally classified her. She had that special European grand air that is characteristic of many of the European and Russian royalty. I was told that she was personally responsible for all the beautiful flowers and flowering bushes that surround the Fischbach chateau, making it look like a fairy palace.

We recalled the times she and her family spent in the United States at the beginning of World War II, as guests of President Roosevelt. She thought, of course, that he was wonderful. I told her that when I was painting his portrait in 1943 he spoke of her arrival and said he was rather uncertain about all the court etiquette and protocol, but I did not tell her how bluntly he expressed it. Roosevelt had more than his fill in taking care of exiled European royalty during World War II.*

WILLIAM TUBMAN

One afternoon, shortly before Christmas 1955, I came back from New York to Locust Valley and was informed that Mr. Harvey Firestone, Jr., had been trying to reach me all day. I had first met the Firestones in 1938 when Mrs. Firestone invited me to Akron to paint her son, a paraplegic, then four years old. I later did several other portraits of the family,

*See chapter 3.

including an enormous oil painting of Harvey Firestone, Sr., that hung in the Firestone Building at the World's Fair. I also painted many boardroom portraits of Firestone executives. Over the years we had become good friends.

When I finally contacted Mr. Firestone, he was just about to leave for the airport but I got his message: a request to go to Liberia and paint President William Tubman, and could I give my answer now as it had to be cabled to Monrovia the next day. As usual, acting upon impulse, I said yes.

Mr. Firestone seemed happy and said, "I love you for that!"

Soon after, Mr. Firestone and I met in New York to discuss the details. The portrait was to be a gift from the Firestone Company to Liberia on the occasion of the third inaugural of President Tubman and was to hang in the new capitol building. It had to be an oil painting, life-size. I shuddered at the thought, as at that time I felt I had not yet acquired enough skill in oil painting, having always used my watercolor medium. All I could think of was the famous portrait of Henri Cristophe, the black emperor of Haiti. But after talking things over with Mr. Firestone, I decided it was not as crazy as most of my friends thought.

I was going to Rome in March where, with a friend, I had rented a villa for the spring, and I could fly easily from there to Monrovia. All the painting material—canvas, easel, and so on—would be flown out from New York, and Mr. Firestone promised that everything would be taken care of. There would be nothing for me to do except walk on a red carpet and then paint.

I began my journey from Rome as planned, and at the airport in Lisbon the red carpet began unrolling. I stayed there for a day, a representative of the company taking care of all the details. The endless flight along the coast of Africa was

Harvey Firestone, Jr.

uneventful until midnight when we reached Roberts Field near Harbel in a raging thunderstorm. I descended from the plane into a veritable Turkish bath. I could hardly breathe in that tropical humidity after the fresh coolness of Rome.

I was met by a group of Firestone people, including Mr. Wilson, the president of the Liberian branch of the company, and his wife. From the airport we drove to Harbel, the headquarters of the company. In the dark it seemed like driving in Central Park in New York, with beautifully paved roads lined with trees. The Wilsons' residence was a spacious plantation-type house, surrounded by what seemed to me a jungle. And the next thing I knew, I was sitting in their cozy, charming living room, drinking vodka and discussing our plans for the next day.

In the morning, after a night of tropical heat in a bed draped with a net to keep out the mosquitos, which felt like a cocoon, Mr. Wilson flew me, in a small plane, to the Monrovia airport. From there we drove to the executive mansion. I looked around and saw that everybody was black; there were a great many uniforms, but the atmosphere was friendly and I felt at ease. Passing through many official rooms, most of them air-conditioned, we entered a drawing room with stuffed red furniture and lots of artificial white flowers in crystal vases. In a few minutes, my future subject appeared. Mr. Firestone had told me what a delightful person he was, and sure enough, I was instantly charmed by him. He had a fine intelligent face with a ready smile and very paintable features. He was immaculately dressed in a light tan suit and tie to match, with the red touch of the French Legion of Honor in his lapel. With him was Mrs. Tubman. She was quite beautiful, with light skin and a profile like Nefertiti's. Her shyness was obvious. She never uttered a word, never smiled, and eventually vanished into space.

As usual, I had no idea what the portrait would be like. I told him at the time that my approach was always with a blank mind and a prayer. After showing me some previous paintings of himself with all the presidential attributes, he expressed the wish to be painted the way he was dressed that morning. Standing by the table, on which he put his right hand, and holding his cigar in his left, he made a perfect composition for a portrait, and I also decided that the cigar was a must.

Before leaving New York, I had gone to the Frick Art Reference Library (the creation of this amazing and unique institution was the idea of Helen Clay Frick) to see reproductions of paintings of black men. At my request, a variety of photographs of different interpretations of men with dark skins were produced. I liked a painting by Reynolds of a handsome Negro in a powdered wig and silk coat with an unfinished background of clouds, and another of a man standing with his hand placed on a marble balustrade. Those two portraits gave me a definite inspiration, so I made a quick sketch on a small board that I took with me. In the background I put the capitol, palm trees, and the sky with huge clouds. Later, I discovered that in Liberia the clouds were indeed enormous and solid white.

I had brought with me as a present for President Tubman a deed for an acre on the moon. They had been issued by the former director of the New York Planetarium for the purpose of collecting funds to build a planetarium on Long Island. Originally they were perfectly legal quitclaim deeds selling for one dollar, but later they were being sold in Rome for speculative prices. The Securities and Exchange Commission decided that they were really securities and as such misleading, and the planetarium had to stop issuing them.

I told the president that I was sure he had everything he

wanted in his country but I was certain that an acre on the moon he did not have! He was delighted with my present and laughed so heartily as he read the contents of the deed that I was sorry I had done it; it interfered with catching a more serious expression on his face. However, I got the likeness, as it generally happens, from the first sitting. I was surprised; I had never painted anyone with a dark skin before and was unfamiliar with the mixing of the colors.

During the five sittings I needed for the likeness, I had a wonderful time with Mr. Tubman. I had learned from the Firestone people that although he was born in Liberia, he was the son of a minister who had come from Atlanta, Georgia. He was quite religious, constantly using Bible texts in his public addresses. I saw a photograph of him in a magazine where he was on his knees delivering a speech. In talking with me he mentioned that shortly before my arrival some Soviet officials had visited Monrovia. Liberia at the time did not recognize the Soviet regime, but he thought that they were charming people. Of course, I said, the Russian people are delightful in general but I could not see how he himself could deal with a Godless government. He seemed to be impressed with what I had said and I felt sure that I had dropped a pearl. (Years later, in the summer of 1971, while painting a portrait of Robert O. Thomas, president of Firestone Tire and Rubber Company, I recounted this conversation and asked if diplomatic relations had since been established with the Soviet Union. The answer was no.)

During one sitting we spoke of the drums that played every night in the distance, and I remembered that my grandson Nicholas, then around fourteen, had asked me to bring back a drum, but so far I had not seen one in the native shops. President Tubman said he would see that I got one. I was a

William V. S. Tubman, President of Liberia

little embarrassed but quite touched by his kind thought. I was very careful not to have him sit for me too long, particularly during the first sitting, and we parted, I believed, before he actually got bored.

I returned happily to the Firestone guest cottage where I was staying while in Monrovia, a charming and comfortable house overlooking the ocean with a view of all the embassies located along the beach. With my hosts, the former president of the Firestone Bank (which was later closed) Mr. Banzer and his wife, I went to many parties given by the president and representatives of different countries. I was quite amazed by the elegance and formality of these receptions. The men wore gray top hats and cutaways at noon and white ties and dashing uniforms at night. The women wore the most stylish dresses made by the best European houses. I was rather appalled by my scanty wardrobe. In Rome I had bartered a portrait in exchange for some dresses from one of the foremost designers, but even so, I had really nothing appropriate to wear! I soon got accustomed to seeing more dark faces than white at those gatherings and frankly enjoyed myself thoroughly.

Through the Banzers I met Miss Angie Brooks, the assistant secretary of state, who later held an important post at the United Nations. Her gay disposition and rather plump appearance seemed incongruent with her responsible role in the cabinet. She told me that she grew the biggest pineapples in her garden and promised to give me one before I left.

As the painting progressed I was now sure it would be a success. I was grateful for the air-conditioning in the executive mansion where I was painting, because the heat and humidity were terrific and the guest house was not air-conditioned. But by the end of the day, with the painting and the parties, I was so exhausted that I did not mind either the humidity or the continuous distant sound of the drums that went on every night. It was explained that the natives used their drums for wakes, weddings, or whatever. It was really more restful than disturbing.

When I got to the final details of the portrait, I asked if I could have one of the president's cigars to copy. It was brought to me by his secretary, Colonel Leigh, a very obliging, talkative man from Martinique, with firm, chiseled features and quite a distinguished appearance. He paid me several visits during the course of my work and told me many interesting things about Monrovia. He was most helpful in many ways and quite cordial, in spite of the fact that I insulted him unknowingly by once mispelling his name in a note written to him. It was "Leigh" and not "Lee"! He had been a medical student, but through some financial reverses had to give up his studies. He did not lose his interest in medicine, however, and observed the unusual treatment of diseases by the natives. He told me that some of their cures of cancer, cataracts, and whatnot were quite inexplicable. He could never find out whether it was the use of herbs or plain witchcraft because the natives were bound to a mysterious secrecy regarding the remedies. I remembered that I had some books on the use of herbs in medicine and I told him that when I returned to the United States I would send him a little present, never thinking that this innocent promise would later bring a sour note to our acquaintance.

After I returned home Colonel Leigh wrote me an unbelievably eloquent letter praising Mr. Firestone's generosity and my talent in the most superlative terms. The portrait, he said, was so great that it was worth much more than the grotesquely exaggerated sum that I was, supposedly, paid. (It was the era of the $64,000 Question on television in the

United States. This is the only explanation I can give for this sum being given as the cost of the portrait in a newspaper account that Colonel Leigh sent to me.) At the end he mentioned my promise of a little present, expressing his hope that I would send him a few thousand dollars in appreciation for his services! I sent the letter to Mr. Firestone and took his advice by sending Colonel Leigh the books on herb medicine as I had promised, and that was that.

After two weeks, as I had promised, the portrait was finished, by noon. I had to leave for Rome at midnight. When we parted, Mr. Tubman expressed his complete approval of the painting and said that he would expect me for the investiture at four o'clock. Apparently I was to be decorated with some order. I was quite overwhelmed. I packed my things and drove to the mansion around four. All the cars were heading in the same direction, some with diplomats in formal uniforms, even African chiefs in golden robes. I could hardly believe my eyes. We were ushered to the main reception room, which was now filled with people sitting around small tables. The portrait, covered with a white sheet, was placed on an easel between two windows. I was seated at a large table between the president and the vice-president, and the elaborate meal started. During the course of the dinner, Mr. Tubman suddenly remembered his promise about the drum and gave a whispered order to one of the attendants standing behind us. In a short while I noticed a great commotion in the adjacent room. It drew the attention of the president. More whispering went on and suddenly he burst into loud laughter. Then, turning to me, he explained that his order was misunderstood and a whole band of drummers had arrived, ready to start the noise!

Finally the president rose and everyone quieted down. He gave a short address, introducing me and complimenting me upon my work, then he pinned the decoration on my shoulder. It was the Humane Order of African Redemption. Now it was my turn to say a few words of general appreciation for the president's kindness and patience. As the applause continued, the portrait was unveiled. I must admit it did look all right and the general excitement was quite tremendous. After President Tubman and I were photographed next to the portrait, we started saying our good-byes. And then Colonel Leigh brought the drum! It was a very rare and old instrument, all tied up in national ribbons. I was so touched by everything that I was speechless.

The flight to Dakar was ghastly, with rain and lightning all the way. What made it all the more uncomfortable was that I had to hold the president's drum and the huge pineapple that Angie Brooks sent at the last minute!

President Tubman died in the summer of 1971 and I felt really sad when the news reached me. He was a great leader and a remarkable man. I felt I had been extremely privileged to have painted him. That fall I attended a service given in his memory at the New York Cultural Center, a very touching and warm affair. His son, a senator, was present and I had a chat with him. I mentioned, among other things, what fun I had with his father regarding the deed on the moon. He told me that he remembered that deed very well and that his father many times jokingly boasted that he was the only one in Liberia to have real estate on the moon. I reminded him that, according to the deed, you had to get to the moon to personally claim your acre. He laughed and said he might consider becoming an astronaut.

Thomas J. Watson, Sr.

Lady Bird Johnson
(official White House portrait)

Lyndon B. Johnson
(official White House portrait)

Hoffman Nickerson

Dr. Mathilde Krim

Dorothy Hutton
(Mrs. E. F. Hutton)

Mrs. Peter Grace and daughters

Victoria Ward Singer
(author's granddaughter)

CHAPTER THREE

FDR's Unfinished Portrait

Of the many portraits I have painted, the last one of Franklin Delano Roosevelt stands out because of the circumstances surrounding the painting and the personality of the subject. Many years have passed since that bright April morning in 1945, when, so suddenly, so dramatically, the sitting was ended and the portrait remained unfinished. But, possibly, it was finished enough to convey a message to those who were to look into those eyes, a message that anyone could interpret in his own way.

Since that time, many memoirs and books have been written about President Roosevelt by his associates and close friends. I believe that I can contribute something to this collection of writings, having painted him twice and having been the last person to speak with him in that final hour of his life. I had written my recollections of painting FDR soon after his death, but did not feel that it was desirable to have them put into print at that time. I had no use for more unnecessary publicity, and if they were published they would reveal a name that so far had been only casually mentioned and which I did not wish to be the first to bring out.

In 1966, however, there appeared a book entitled *The Time Between the Wars* by Jonathan Daniels in which a short mention of Lucy Rutherfurd produced a sudden furor. Newspapers and magazines joined in a series of articles regarding her association with FDR. I was pestered with telephone calls and finally, very reluctantly, at the request of the Rutherfurd family, I released a photograph of the portrait of Lucy I had painted in 1937. This was reproduced in *Life* magazine in September. I was utterly miserable. Some articles in the press were correct, some rather inaccurate, but none really gave the true picture. In 1968 a second book appeared by the same author, entitled *Washington Quadrille,* and conveyed to me an even less accurate picture of Lucy as I knew her, but I realized that Mr. Daniels had never met her and it was like painting a portrait from a photograph of a person you had never known. Now I felt that it was time to concentrate on my own impressions, and as I made that decision, I recalled an afternoon in June 1945.

It was the first time since that fateful day of FDR's passing that Lucy and I had seen each other and were able to talk over the events we had shared. After a luncheon at the Hotel Pierre, we went to her suite and continued our conversation. I sat on the window seat and Lucy collapsed on the bed. Her eyes were red from crying. I don't know how we got through that luncheon. So many, many things to talk over!

"I have burned all his letters," she said suddenly.

"Oh Lucy, you could not have done that!"

"But why? It does not concern anyone!"

"It does, it will later."

"No, no!" Lucy insisted.

"Someday," I said, it is bound to come out and it might not be in the right way. You know, Lucy, I have it all written down, because in the years to come it should be known the way it was."

"I don't mind what you have written because I trust you, but I do not wish anything to be brought out while I am alive!"

I saw her several more times before she died in 1948, but we never discussed the subject again. However, her consent to my eventually publishing my recollections of painting FDR and of her association with him gave me the incentive to go very carefully through my notes regarding my encounters with Roosevelt, review everything that was written about that time, and compare notes with some of the persons involved.

I may have produced a one-sided picture, but I felt that those two remarkable characters, Lucy and Roosevelt, should be presented not only from the point of view of political associates and the press, but also by an artist who had the opportunity to study them both at different times and in many ways.

LUCY RUTHERFURD

The first I ever heard of FDR was when he was elected governor of New York State. The fact that he had risen above his affliction and was determined to lead an active life in politics in spite of his polio made it impossible not to admire him. Later, I began to change my mind. He was running for president and I was on the Republican side. With every new election he won, I was less and less enthusiastic and actually not happy with him at all.

In 1937, when I was doing some work in Aiken, South Carolina, I heard, for the first time, directly about FDR and Lucy. I was told by some of the people I met there that a Mrs. Winthrop Rutherfurd, who stayed in Aiken for the winter months, and of whom everyone spoke with affection and ad-

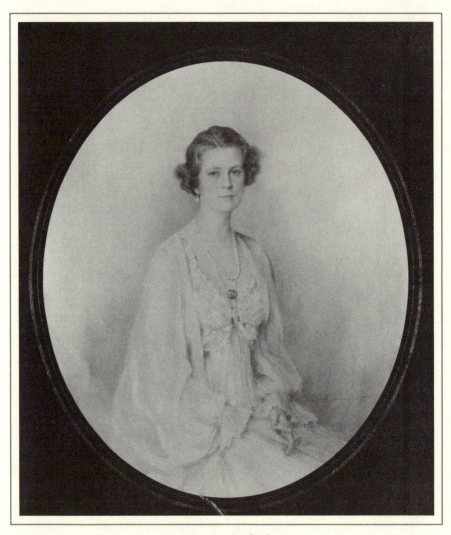

Lucy Rutherfurd

miration, had been romantically involved with Roosevelt many years ago, before her marriage to Mr. Rutherfurd.

I was staying at the Wilcox Inn when, one day, an extremely tall, good-looking young girl came to see me. She was Alice Rutherfurd and she said that she was very anxious to have a portrait of her mother. She spoke of her so affectionately that I was surprised later to discover that Lucy Rutherfurd was her stepmother. All five stepchildren were truly devoted to her. I was invited to their home the next day.

I believe that it will not be exaggerating to say that meeting Lucy Rutherfurd for the first time was quite impressive. Very tall, like the rest of her family, exquisitely lovely and gracious, she impressed you not so much by her striking appearance as by the shining quality in her features, particularly in her smile. She wore clothes that made her look somewhat older, as if deliberately diminishing the thirty years difference between herself and her husband. However, the graceful, flowing tea gowns she wore at night were so becoming that I had little hesitation in later choosing one of them, of turquoise chiffon, for my painting.

I was asked first to paint a portrait of her husband. Winthrop Rutherfurd, in spite of his advanced years, was one of the handsomest men I have ever painted, and certainly the most aristocratic. He looked like an English peer with his chiseled features, sharp eyes, and a sarcastic expression around his mouth; yet there was something about his face that vaguely resembled FDR. Lucy, at one time, admitted this herself. As I learned later, he had been madly in love with Consuelo Vanderbilt, and in her book *The Glitter and the Gold* (1952), she referred to him as "Mr. R." or the "Rosenkavalier," because he always sent her roses. However, it ended very dramatically for both, as she was forced to marry the duke of Marlborough, whom she later divorced.

I liked Mr. Rutherfurd right away, and although warned by his wife that he did not hesitate in saying sharp things, we got along beautifully.

We had a mutual interest in fox terriers. Mr. Rutherfurd, the owner of a famous kennel, was interested in the breed, while my interest was of a more personal nature. In our house in Locust Valley we had a delightful fox terrier by the name of Ezra who reminded me of an equally entrancing specimen named Bobick we had had many years before in Russia. Ezra was sired by the famous champion Brass Tacks, and so Mr. Rutherfurd introduced me to all the details of fox terrier history. Even before I finished the portrait, it was planned that I should do another small picture of him in Allamuchy, their New Jersey estate, with fox terriers bouncing around him. I saw right away the responsibility of such an undertaking.

When the portrait was finished, I was not pleased with it. Mr. Rutherfurd was in very frail health, and I am sure had much more vitality than I could see at the time, and this is what I felt I had missed. He was the object of constant care and attention. The devotion that Lucy showed him every minute was one of the outstanding features of their life. Everything whirled around him; their life was governed by his invalid regime. She never went out in the evenings and completely devoted her existence to making him happy and comfortable. I did a much better portrait of Lucy. With a subject like her, it could not be otherwise, and I believe I did catch something of her fascinating personality.

As the sittings went on, with the conversation being mostly about our children and mutual friends, I got to know Lucy to a certain degree. She was not an expansive person, but gentle and kindly, interested only in others. Her serenity seemed to be mostly on the surface; I felt that her mind was constantly preoccupied with her husband's welfare. I learned that she married Mr. Rutherfurd in her late twenties (she was in her middle forties at the time). She acquired a family of five children, a girl and four boys. I am sure it was not easy for her at the beginning to establish the wonderful relationship that existed between them later. I can say truly I have seldom seen a mother more beloved and respected than was Lucy by her stepchildren. She had one daughter of her own, Barbara, who was a frail, rather skinny girl of fourteen, wearing glasses, with features that promised to be much better looking later on.

Lucy asked me about my children. I told her a lot about them and how lucky I was to have our wonderful Tatassia, who was everything to all of us and left me in complete peace of mind when I had to be away from home. I said how complicated it was sometimes to keep up my activities as a mother of three lively children and as an artist overloaded with commissions. I mentioned that I hoped to bring some little gifts to my family upon my return home, but thought I would hardly find the time to do it. When I came to say good-bye to her a few days later, she had a beautifully wrapped package ready with presents for all my children, and a lovely blue scarf for Tatassia, "because she is young," Lucy added. Tatassia was over sixty!

This was the introduction to a wonderful friendship that grew as the years went by. I painted several of the children later, and also Mr. Rutherfurd, with the pups. That was a tough picture to do—he was determined to have the exact details of canine anatomy, and all Lucy wanted was a characteristic silhouette of him and the dogs on the lawn.

To paint that picture of Mr. Rutherfurd and a half-dozen fox terriers, I had to have some good snapshots. I asked a photographer, Mr. Robbins, to come to Allamuchy for that purpose. Mr. Robbins was a very nice Russian gentleman whom I had known for a number of years. Before the Russian Revolution, he had considerable property in the Crimea and was always interested in photography. He was introduced to me in New York as an amateur photographer. I always like to have snaps made when I paint my portraits. Some artists, I believe, do not consider it to be real art, but I consider it very important, particularly for my watercolor medium. You cannot change a thing, and an immortalization of certain positions and lines is essential. Besides, it enables me to study different poses and expressions before starting the actual work. Mr. Robbins was introduced to me for this purpose, but later he showed his amazing ability as a photographer in reproducing my paintings to perfection.

Mr. Robbins was a rather short, grayish man in his late fifties, at that time, with a pince-nez on his nose. His real name was Nicholas Kotzubinsky, but the judge, upon giving him his naturalization papers, advised him to simplify his name for practical purposes, and he reduced it to Kobbins. Unfortunately, the *K* in his handwriting looked very much like an *R* so he became "Robbins." He was a character, and I always felt guilty for getting irritated with him or for making fun of him. He was essentially a most loyal and respectful gentleman, but his ability to argue was impossible.

Being single, at that time, he had quite an eye for the ladies, and when he met Lucy, he really got carried away. I later received a letter from him which I am sorry I did not keep. It was the most elaborate eulogy to her, and on several pages he wrote how deeply he was impressed with her spiritual and physical beauty. At the time I thought it a little funny, but now I see it in another light. It is significant to me that she could evoke in a man that type of devotion. Lucy was very feminine; she had no extraordinary intellect, but she possessed the most idealistic, almost naive, mind, with a really unselfish, understanding heart. She was a true Christian and in all our religious talks, I never once sensed the difference in our creeds—she being Roman Catholic, and I Russian Orthodox. In her presence, you always felt uplifted and inspired for the best.

I certainly enjoyed staying with the Rutherfurds at Allamuchy. They had a big old-fashioned house with a chapel, set on a lake in the beautiful hills of New Jersey. There were endless roads on which wild deer frequently appeared.

One moonlit evening, Lucy and I went driving along the woodland roads and somehow the name of Roosevelt was mentioned.

"You know him?" It was more of a statement than a question.

"Oh, very well." There was almost a reverence in her tone.

When I was in Aiken I had paid little attention to the rather vague rumors about some early romantic association between Lucy and the president. I certainly did not realize there was any continuation of that friendship between the two. I felt just a bit amazed.

"There is one question I would like to ask, Lucy. Tell me, is he sincere?" That he lacked sincerity was one point upon which most of my friends were unanimous, while my own thoughts about him were inconclusive. Her answer was most affirmative, but it still did not convince me. She continued talking about Roosevelt in admiring terms. So many qualities were brought up that I do not remember them all. We discussed his extraordinary ability to work, his dynamic approach to anything he undertook, and his greatness in general. This conversation did not develop any further because, in all honesty, I could not join in her enthusiasm. It was only years later, in the midst of the war, that his name was brought up again.

THE FIRST PORTRAIT

In early spring 1943, I was busy with more portraits in Aiken. Naturally, I saw Lucy. Mr. Rutherfurd by that time was a bed-ridden invalid. I saw him once for a few minutes. Several days before leaving Aiken, I came to say good-bye to Lucy. As we were sitting in the living room drinking tea, she began to talk about my painting and the ability I had to catch a likeness. "You should really paint the president," she said. "He has such a remarkable face. There is no painting of him that gives his true expression. I think you could do a wonderful portrait, and he would be such an interesting person to paint! Would you do a portrait of him if it was arranged?"

While she was talking, I had visions of entering the White House with all my paraphernalia, painting under the most strenuous conditions, and possibly producing a monstrosity.

"It would be quite an undertaking," I said. "I really don't know what to say. How could it be arranged?"

"Oh, that could be done if you really want to."

One more moment of hesitation and I accepted the challenge.

The following morning Lucy called me at the Wilcox Inn in Aiken. She had telephoned Washington, and the president said he would sit for his portrait in two weeks. I was stunned. I went at once to see Lucy. I did not understand how the whole thing could have been arranged so quickly. Although there had been more rumors about her continuing friendship with FDR, I did not think, at that time, that she actually talked with him or saw him. I was also surprised that Roosevelt had agreed to pose so soon for his portrait—he had just returned from Casablanca and I did not see how he could find time for the sittings. When I expressed these doubts to Lucy, she said, "Oh, I told him that he could continue his work while you painted, and that you worked very fast and would not require too much of his time. He said he could give you two mornings."

There was no backing out. I was trapped into something I had neither wished for nor planned. My first concern was where I would stay. It was wartime and I knew that every space in Washington was filled. After several futile efforts, I decided to call Mrs. Richard Mellon. I had done some portraits for her and had stayed several times in her big house in Georgetown. I told her that I had an important commission in Washington and was in a desperate state because I had nowhere to stay. She kindly agreed to put me up, and in two weeks I appeared at their house. When I told them whom I was painting, the Mellons were astonished. They had thought my subject might be Madame Chiang Kai-shek.

I called the White House right away and Grace Tully, the president's secretary, said he was expecting me. The following morning I collected my painting equipment—a portfolio with drawing boards, pencils, brushes, and the silver paint box which I always carried in my purse. I was driven by Mr. Mellon's chauffeur. We were stopped at the White House gate, but let through after a call to Miss Tully. I was nervous as I walked through the big reception hall filled with waiting people. A very nice man, Mr. [William D.] Simmons, took me under his wing, and after waiting a few moments in some conference room, led me into the inner sanctum. I suddenly remembered someone saying that when you enter the president's office, he greets you with such friendliness that his hand seems to stretch across the entire room. It was true, when I saw his smile and the familiar face, and heard the still more familiar voice, I knew that Lucy must have spoken well of me. One of his first questions was: "How is Mrs. Rutherfurd? And how is Barbara?"

I decided on the pose immediately. Since the president was sitting at his desk, I had little choice. A few moments of the most tremendous activity followed—chairs were pushed, curtains drawn up and down, a quick snapshot of the pose was taken, and finally we were settled. The president was wearing a gray suit and a blue tie. He was very cheerful, perfectly unconcerned about the whole thing, and I perched rather uncomfortably on a chair, ready to start the sketch.

"I had a portrait done some time ago," the president began, "by a Mexican artist who called it *The Fireside Chat*. There I was, sitting by a fireplace with two little cactus plants on the sides for Mexican atmosphere, and the red glow of the fire reflecting on my face. All *I* could name it was *R. in Hell!*"

That broke the ice for me and I told my little story about Pope Leo XIII who, after having had his picture done, was asked by the pious artist to write a text from the Bible on his portrait. Without hesitation he wrote, "It is I; be not afraid." I said I hoped this would not be necessary with mine.

Before starting the painting I decided not to mention the war or the Russian situation, past or the present. I would let the president do all the talking. He spoke of visiting various countries in Europe, and the topic of European royalty came up. He seemed preoccupied by the presence in the United States of many royal refugees, but because he had created the problem himself, he did not know what to do about it.

When war clouds began to gather over Europe, he had

thought the polite thing to do was to write nice little notes to all the heads of the governments whose countries were threatened and in danger: "I'm so sorry, is there anything I can do?" The first to reply was Grand Duchess Charlotte of Luxembourg who said she would like to come to America. "Come along," he answered. He went to greet her, he said, and for once was quite speechless. She had arrived with her husband and seven children, none of whom he knew she had. They were penniless and expected FDR to support them in the style to which they were accustomed.

"I soon put an end to that idea," he said. "I gave them some money to start with, but now they are living on rich American and European friends. However, Lotti [Charlotte] is still a source of trouble for she keeps writing whining complaints about the fact that there is not enough fuss made over her presence here."

The Norwegians, Roosevelt said, were almost as bad. They lived very simply somewhere in Virginia. They had no money problems, but they were very pompous and assumed that he, "dear Franklin," was trying to reform them by pooh-poohing all the fuss and feathers and formal etiquette they observed. Queen Wilhelmina of Holland was a continual problem, he said, because she had no sense of humor and kept getting offended. The worse offense was caused by a caricature in *Vogue* of all the exiled rulers done (as I recall) by the Russian artist Alajalov. Roosevelt said that he sent copies to all the people pictured therein; . . . all received it in the proper spirit except Wilhelmina and King Haakon of Norway. They both were offended and had been cool ever since.

"If they keep this up," FDR continued, "I'll be 'Uncle Franklin' to every royal house in Europe. I don't see what they expect to gain by it." Moreover, he said, "the royalty are a problem because they refuse to adapt to a changing world. They expect to be reinstated after the war, but that is doubtful. In many cases their subjects feel they have been deserted, and after the war they may prefer entirely different political setups."

"He asked about my background in Russia, which I answered as briefly as possible, being busy with my sketch. He said he was sorry he . . . never visited Russia although he had traveled a great deal in Europe.

"When I was in Berlin," he said, "I was imprisoned for a few hours." Obviously amused by the startled expression on my face, he proceeded with the story. It seems that he, his mother, and a friend of hers were seated in a compartment of a railroad car heading for Berlin. At one of the last stops, a Prussian officer stepped in and took a place in the corner. Without a word, the officer suddenly got up and closed the nearby window. Mrs. Roosevelt's friend said that she had a bad headache and wished the window opened. When young Franklin did her bidding, the Prussian officer promptly closed the window again. In silence Roosevelt repeated the procedure. When the Prussian got up for the third time, FDR fought him back to his seat, knocking him to the floor in the process. The officer rose and took his seat. There was complete silence until the train pulled into the Berlin station. After the usual excitement of leaving the train, getting a porter, and organizing the luggage, Franklin was suddenly seized by a policeman and put in jail.

"My mother called the American embassy, but it took them several hours to get me out of prison," the president concluded.

By this time I had finished with my sketch. According to the wishes of the president, it was to be a small portrait, twelve inches by ten, exactly the size of the picture of my youngest daughter which I had brought with me and which stood on his desk while I worked.

"Russians seem to like doing small paintings," said FDR, looking at my daughter's picture. "Take your icons for instance, the detailed work. I had two icons given to me by Mr. [Joseph] Davies [then the American ambassador to Russia]. He brought them from Russia, but somehow they don't seem to look like others I have seen."

"I am sure my brother Andrey would know what they are," I said. "He is quite an authority on icons."

"Well, someday you will both come to Hyde Park for luncheon and he might look at them."

As I finished my sketch, I felt that his gray suit and blue tie were too drab for a painting. I told him how sorry I was not to put more glamour into it. Laughing, the president said that the best he could do to help me would be to wear his favorite Navy cape. When the cape was produced I added it to the sketch and put a few gray clouds in the background. The effect was entirely different, and when I left I was more or less satisfied with what I had accomplished at that sitting.

The next day I arrived at the same time at the White House gate. By now I felt completely at ease, did not wear a hat, and even forgot to take any identification. When asked for credentials by the guards, I took my paint box from my purse and said that I had an appointment to paint the president's portrait. I'm afraid my paint box was unimpressive because they then checked with Miss Tully.

FDR greeted me with such genuine friendliness that it helped me more than anything to work quickly on his portrait. I got a magnificent start right away. As usual, I verified my work by looking at it in a little jade mirror that is part of my painting equipment. (Mrs. Harvey S. Firestone gave it to me, and I never paint without it.) The president thought this very funny. I was aware of his amused expression, but it was not the one I wished to put on the portrait. Too many pictures of him show his "presidential" smile, and an expression of earnest seriousness seemed to me more desirable. Afterward, he looked through the mirror at the picture, as it is the only way people will really see the likeness in their portraits. He thought it was fine, and I continued at top speed while the president chatted and smoked cigarettes. I smoked also, and once in a while he would light my cigarette. The conversation caught up with yesterday's on traveling in Europe. He told me that his father, as a young man, was sent to Europe for a year with two thousand dollars in his pocket. It seems he spent that money before the year was over, so he proceeded to travel by foot. In Italy he met a delightful Jesuit priest with whom he could exchange a few words in Latin, and together they reached Naples just at the time when Garibaldi and his troops were engaged in their successful revolt against the Neapolitan regime. As the young man had nothing much to do, not having a cent in his pockets, he joined the revolutionaries, and for a short time wore their uniform.

Later, the president came to talk about Maxim Litvinoff, who was then serving as the ambassador from the USSR.

"At one time," he said, "I received information that for political reasons the Soviet government had granted free worship and permission to build mosques in one of the Moslem republics subordinated to Russia. I said to Litvinoff, 'Look here, Max, how is it that you do not allow free worship in Russia, and grant it to people in Asia?'"

Litvinoff seemed surprised that Roosevelt knew about it, and said something about how it was for purely political reasons and that, after all, religion was not important.

"How can you say that when you were trained to be a rabbi?" the president asked.

Amazed at Roosevelt's knowledge, Litvinoff said he was not interested in that subject at all.

"Don't you believe in God?"

Litvinoff said he did not believe in anything.

"Now listen, Max. There will come a time when you will be regretful. One of these days you are going to die, and as you are dying you will suddenly feel a great need for God and you will believe in Him. But your last moments will be miserable for you'll not be sure if it won't be too late. Don't you think that it is better to make peace with your Maker now instead of waiting until the last moment when it is too late?"

Litvinoff said nothing but later remarked to Cordell Hull, the secretary of state, "You know, your president made me feel very uncomfortable. He makes me think about things I don't want to think about."

Later a mystified Hull repeated the remark to Roosevelt, who explained its meaning. Thereafter, whenever FDR saw Litvinoff he gave him that "Max, remember your dying day!" look and Litvinoff always looked most uncomfortable.

Was the story correct, or exaggerated for fun? I do not know, but we had a good laugh.

Another topic we discussed was the present state of the nation and the role of the president. FDR said that the most important thing about being president was to keep one's sense of balance and perspective. "Some people think that a lot of things I do are unbalanced, and they probably do seem so if one thinks only in terms of the present. But I'm thinking of twenty-five years from now." He said that most people in this country, particularly the rich, have not awakened to the fact that life will never be like it was in the past.

When the appointment hour ended, I still had a few

touches on the face to make and of course the cape was hardly blocked in. As I had no snaps of the cape, I had to do the whole thing from life, which meant a great deal more time. The president had given me only those two mornings for the painting. I began begging for another appointment. Miss Tully was asked to come in. She firmly said that tomorrow was out of the question, that there was this and that and the Congress besides.

"Grace, I will cut the time of luncheon and we can salvage half an hour," the president said.

I asked if anybody else could pose for the cape. Miss Tully said she would arrange that. The next day was a hurried sitting, but the likeness was so good, and the president was so pleased, that he kept Congress waiting ten minutes until the face was finished. He took one quick look through my mirror and was completely satisfied.

After that I moved, with all my belongings, to the Constitution Room and the nice Mr. Simmons appeared wearing the cape. He was tall and broad-shouldered, very much in stature like the president. At least an hour and a half passed before I finished painting the heavy black material, always a difficult thing for watercolor, and disentangled the complicated design of the silk frog that held the cape together. I remember how extraordinarily alike was the president's and Mr. Simmon's build. Mr. Simmons told me that once he actually had to wear the cape in the president's car. It was pouring rain and the president did not feel well. The crowds, he said, never knew whom they cheered.

When I finished the painting, Miss Tully and a number of people came in to look at it. There seemed to be no flaw. As I think of it now, however, I agree with Bill Hasset, one of FDR's secretaries, who said that it was "too pretty." Someone

Franklin D. Roosevelt, 1943

expressed regret that the portrait was not larger, to which the president replied that someday he would ask me to do another, life-size, for the White House or Hyde Park.

A week later I had to go back to Aiken to complete some unfinished work. Lucy was delighted with the president's picture, which I had placed in a very effective antique mirror frame. Roosevelt had expressed to her his desire to have color prints of the portrait to give to his friends. I began this task upon my return to New York and as soon as I had something to show, I called Miss Tully and she made an appointment for me with FDR. Again I appeared at the president's office, this time with the framed portrait and proofs of the prints. He was all praise.

"It seems as if there should be a horizon of water," I said. I was thinking, actually, of Washington in his cape, crossing the Delaware, and mumbled words to that effect. The president, either jokingly or seriously (I do not know which) said. "Well, we'll call this one *Signing the Atlantic Charter.*"

This particular episode had reached its conclusion, and I had succeeded in painting FDR to his entire satisfaction. While it was Lucy's idea, I did it on my own and personally presented it as a gift to the president, contrary to some notions expressed in later years that it was commissioned by Lucy. But I am very grateful to her for having made this rather unusual and unexpected experience possible. I was, by now, completely charmed by the president and continued to be more so as time went by, to the utter amazement of my Republican friends.

HYDE PARK

On a Saturday afternoon in the middle of July 1943, I returned to Locust Valley from a day's trip to New York, and my old maid Marie announced that I was to call Operator 11, then followed a strange word, and "New York." During the seventeen years that Marie had worked for me, I do not remember her once being correct in giving the names in any telephone message. It was always exciting to find out who had *really* called. Since the "strange word" was not discernible, I had to wait patiently until Operator 11 called again. She did, and the call came from Poughkeepsie, New York. This time I did not blame Marie for the spelling! It was Miss Tully calling from Hyde Park with an invitation from President Roosevelt for my brother and myself to come on Monday for luncheon, stating which train to take from New York. I could not have been more surprised that FDR had kept his promise to invite us to Hyde Park. He hardly ever left Washington, we were in the thick of war, and business affairs seldom allowed him time to relax.

I called up Andrey in Pittsburgh and learned that he was just about to leave for Wyoming on a vacation. In view of the very interesting invitation, he decided to postpone his departure. For years my brother had been anything but an admirer of Roosevelt, and here was his opportunity to confirm or change his opinion.

When we arrived in Poughkeepsie, the presidential car, with an army chauffeur, was waiting for us. Driving through the town the policemen saluted us (or rather the car), and as I reclined in the comfortable limousine, my brother uttered one of his typical remarks. "Now don't get excited, Ellie, they are only taking you for Queen Wilhelmina." The chauffeur must have overheard the remark because when we approached the entrance to the Roosevelt estate he said, "Last week Queen Wilhelmina visited the president. She was a quarter of an hour early, so she decided to wait at this gate."

We drove in and in a few minutes were greeted by Miss

Tully. I was all eyes. My first impression was of an old mansion with great atmosphere. It had rather shabby dignity, beautiful old furniture, and family portraits that made you feel comfortably at ease right away. As Miss Tully took us through the hall to the big living room I noticed and called my brother's attention to Paul Troubetskoy's sculpture of Roosevelt as a young man. The president had told me the story of this work during the sitting in Washington. It seems that when Troubetskoy started it only the bust was planned. Then he went further and did the hands and continued with the legs. For no apparent reason he stopped at the knees. As the sculpture appears now, placed on a square wooden pedestal, it shows a handsome young man—with no legs—almost like an ominous prophecy of the president's future disability.

When, a short time later, Miss Tully said the president was ready to see us, we found him in a tiny little study, sitting with rolled shirt sleeves before a desk piled high with papers. After the exchange of gay greetings, he slid, with great ease, from his armchair to a wheelchair, and we accompanied him through the lower floor, listening to his stories of all the details of the various rooms. We started with the enormous, rather dark living room. The first thing I noticed was a bust of Nicholas Roerich, a Russian artist, on one of the sideboards. I was quite struck by its presence. Roerich was a very mysterious person. Besides being a painter of Russian and Oriental landscape scenes, and creator of the scenario for Nÿinsky's *Sacre du Printemps*, he had a tremendous following as an occult leader. My brother was extremely interested in him, but at one time he discovered that Roerich had plagiarized an Oriental miniature. When Roerich heard of this discovery, he said to a mutual friend, "Does not Avinoff know what dark forces I can put upon him?" Vice-president Henry

Wallace was also immersed in Roerich teachings. Ultimately, Roerich left for India where he later died.

The presence of the bust suggested to me that FDR had been interested in occult matters. Proof of this came from a Russian friend, Colonel Alexei Lvoff (grandson of the composer of the Russian national anthem). He was a remarkable old man in his early nineties, a vegetarian who neither smoked nor drank, and who had all his faculties. He was also a dedicated member of the Theosophical Society. He told me that he greatly admired FDR, and that at one time, listening to a Fireside Chat, he felt that FDR had some connection with one of the secret societies that he, Lvoff, was involved in. Lvoff sent FDR a cryptic question by wire, expecting a yes or no answer. The reply was yes, which confirmed in Lvoff's mind that Roosevelt was a member of this secret society and was interested in mysticism. Roosevelt had never mentioned any of this to me, but I thought of the story as we passed the bust of Roerich.

We then progressed to a charming connecting room called the Dresden Room. It was filled with Dresden china, flowery French chintzes, and many photographs of royal personages.

"My wife wants to change this room to a den." Roosevelt laughed. "She won't have her way this time." When I think of it, I believe this was the only time that I, personally, ever heard him refer to Mrs. Roosevelt.

After passing through several other less impressive rooms, FDR suggested driving us through the grounds. A convertible Ford was waiting at the entrance, and it really was a shock to me to see, for the first time, the president carried by two strong men to the car. He sat at the wheel, inviting me to sit beside him. My brother and Miss Tully took their seats in the back. I believe it was one of the giddiest drives I ever had. The president drove with speed and assurance through the narrow stony roads with many sharp corners, chatting all the time and answering the salutes of sentinels on duty along the way. At one curve he pointed to a butterfly and asked what it was. My brother said right away, "It's a Viceroy, Mr. President."

My brother said that in his wildest dreams he could never have imagined a drive like this, with the president of the United States at the wheel, and his sister giggling nervously in the front seat. And nervous I was, for my only thought at the moment was to get back safely. It flashed through my mind what awful publicity it would be to have an accident under such circumstances! The mad drive continued downhill until we reached the Hudson River. Pointing to the enormous sign on the west bank which marked the location of Father Divine's "Heaven," the president read its message aloud: "PEACE, ISN'T IT WONDERFUL!

After our safe return, the president suggested a visit to the library. We toured the numerous rooms, already a living memorial to FDR. While we were there, the two icons of which the president had spoken while in Washington were brought in. My brother was one of the foremost authorities on icons in this country. He identified the first one as of Polish origin, and the second icon, also not Russian, as St. George and the Dragon.

We moved on to the next room, and suddenly the gentleman who had brought the icons came running after us. "But there is no dragon: it is a man!" he said. My brother was quite startled to discover that he had overlooked such a detail in the icon, perhaps because the icon was so dark. "Then it could not be St. George," he said.

"It might not even be a saint!" the president added.

In a matter of seconds my brother was on the right track.

"Oh, of course, it is St. Demetrius of Thessalonica, but it looked so much like Raphael's St. George that I did not examine the lower part. If you will allow me, Mr. President, I will send you reproductions of other icons of this saint." There was quite a correspondence about this saint and reproductions of icons. Many years later, in the fifties, when we were again in Hyde Park, this correspondence was shown to me by the librarian.

The library of Hyde Park is so well known that I will not describe it, but I will mention the "Chamber of Oddities," a tremendous room in the basement where Roosevelt kept all his caricatures and various odd presents he had received. Originally it was called the "Chamber of Horrors," but one day a man who had presented him with an embroidered cushion with FDR's likeness came to inspect where his present was located, and was shocked and offended by the inscription on the door. It was then that the name was changed to Chamber of Oddities. The things in this room were really funny and odd, and the president enjoyed his cartoons and caricatures immensely. At the end of the room was a fireplace with a tremendous bas-relief of Roosevelt as a sphinx with a cigarette holder in his mouth. It was made during his last campaign when it was not known whether he would say yes or no.

The president turned in his wheelchair and said to my brother: "Dr. Avinoff, you are a director of a museum. Could you tell me to what dynasty this masterpiece belongs?" My brother, without hesitation, said, "Mr. President, I would not know exactly the dynasty, but it seems to have pre-dynastic characteristics!" The president caught on to the joke and burst out laughing. "You certainly hit it!" he said, with a slap on my brother's back.

Elizabeth Shoumatoff with FDR at Hyde Park

Before getting into the car, my brother, who had brought along his camera, insisted upon taking pictures of Roosevelt and myself. When we returned to the house, luncheon was served. The president sat at the head of the table, my brother, Miss Tully, and myself at his right.

The luncheon was delicious. We had the best chicken cream soup, then Polish ham, which the president carved himself with generous second helpings to all. With such talkers as FDR and my brother, the conversation rolled on incessantly. Religion was discussed, chiefly in connection with the situation in Soviet Russia. The predicament seemed to bother the president a lot.

My brother referred to the old sleigh that we had seen in the Hyde Park library. It had been used by FDR's grandparents. Originally, it was the property of Napoleon III, who received it as a present from Emperor Alexander II of Russia. My brother mentioned something about Alexander I and his strange end, and told the story of the murder of his father, Paul I, in 1801. Alexander, who was quite a young man then, was aware of the plot but realizing the menace his father was to the country, did nothing to prevent it. Throughout his entire reign, otherwise a succession of glory and achievement, Alexander carried this burden in his heart and finally, according to rumor, decided to simulate his own death. Many people believed that years later he reappeared in Siberia as a saintly hermit called Feodor Kuzmich. I remember that the president was most impressed with this story. He looked earnestly at my brother saying, "You mean to say that a ruler of a great country could have been proclaimed dead by his people and not die?"

Shortly after FDR died all sorts of rumors began to circulate concerning his end. One book that I received even hinted at the possibility that he never died at all. Of course my brother jokingly insisted, if that were so, that it was he who gave the idea of a simulated death to FDR , who, no doubt, was among the lamas somewhere in Tibet. Wasn't the fact that he had named his secret rural retreat in Maryland "Shangri-La" after the remote mysterious Tibetan monastery in James Hilton's *Lost Horizon* a possible clue to his ultimate destination?

The luncheon finally ended, and we left immediately. When back on the train alone, my brother admitted that he was completely charmed by President Roosevelt!

THE LAST PORTRAIT

In the middle of March 1945, on my way home from Palm Beach, I stopped in Aiken to do some paintings: one was of a little step-grandson of Lucy's. She herself was away at the time and I saw her only for a brief moment when she dropped in at her daughter-in-law's the day before I was leaving for the North.

Mr. Rutherford had died that winter. Lucy was wearing a black dress which enhanced the whiteness of her skin, and she looked perfectly lovely. She had just returned from Washington where she was visiting with her sister.

"There was somebody who asked very much about you," she said in a low voice as we sat in the far end of the living room. "He seems very anxious to have his portrait done now."

"But how does he look?" I asked, feeling a slight shock at the idea, vividly recalling the latest photographs I had seen of FDR. He had just returned from his meeting at Yalta with Churchill and Stalin. "Those last pictures," I added, "seem ghastly."

"He is thin and frail, but there is something about his face that shows more the way he looked when he was young. Having lost so much weight, his features, always handsome, are more definitely chiseled. I think," Lucy continued, in an even lower tone, "if this portrait is painted, it should not be postponed."

I was rather puzzled by the whole thing. Was this Lucy's idea, or did FDR really want it? Then I remembered his telling me about the life-size portrait for the White House at the time I finished the 1943 portrait.

Lucy went on, "He is going to Warm Springs very soon and you could go on the presidential train." This suggestion made me feel even worse about the venture. "Or, you might come back to Aiken and we will drive together." The Georgia Warm Springs Foundation, which FDR had set up in 1927 to treat polio victims, was a favorite presidential retreat; it was only a few hours from Aiken. We parted without any definite plans, except that Lucy would telephone me at Locust Valley.

Easter that year was on April 1, and my brother arrived from Pittsburgh for the holidays. My home was still closed (due to wartime conditions) and I was staying with my daughter Zoric and her husband in Locust Valley. I told my brother what Lucy had said and expressed a complete lack of enthusiasm to go south again when I had just returned from there. It had been a long absence and besides, the idea of painting FDR, who seemed tired and burdened by war responsibilities, did not appeal to me at all. My brother, to the contrary, urged me to accept the challenge, as before. Anyway, I could still wait to decide as I had had no call yet.

Two or three days later, however, Lucy telephoned to say it was all arranged. The president was at Warm Springs ready and waiting. Again, I felt there was no backing out. But a lot of details had to be settled. First, I needed a photographer, as I could hardly count on much time from the president himself, so Mr. Robbins was my natural choice. I called Lucy and asked if she could arrange with Miss Tully for a Mr. Robbins to accompany us. Also, if we motored to Warm Springs, picking up Lucy in Aiken, the acute question of gasoline had to be solved. (Gas was rationed, and train reservations had to be made weeks ahead.) Lucy said that with our combined coupons and possibly the president's help, I need not worry. So my car was put on a low mixture (whatever that meant) in order to progress sixteen miles to a gallon.

Mr. Robbins was still a problem. Miss Tully had to wait for

a decision. Probably he had to be investigated. For my part, I gave him the best reference and I am certainly happy that he never betrayed my trust in him; he kept his mouth shut all these years.

The day of departure was set for Saturday, April 7. None of my friends in Locust Valley knew anything about it, and Mr. Robbins was complete discretion itself. We left early in the morning in my convertible Cadillac sedan. Passing through New York City I decided to stop at the Metropolitan Opera ticket office as I had lost a favorite jeweled clip a few nights before and, after inquiries, it was returned to me. I could not have been more happy and Mr. Robbins said this was a good omen. Of course that statement, in view of future events, could be challenged!

The drive was uneventful. I had stopped smoking for Lent and continued after Easter (I followed the Russian Orthodox Church calendar which made Easter later than for Western churches), so I occupied myself with candy and chewing gum. I was hardly in a pleasant mood. Besides, Mr. Robbins irritated me the whole time, arguing about different routes and directing my driving. Late the next night we reached Aiken. I was so happy to arrive at Lucy's charming house and enjoy, even at this late hour, her cordial hospitality. Mr. Robbins was put up at the Henderson Hotel and Lucy and I sat for a while talking. Lucy was quite excited about the trip to Warm Springs.

"You must take a good night's rest," she said, "and not get up early. We will leave directly after luncheon. The president telephoned that he will meet us in Macon at four o'clock. So we will be in Warm Springs for dinner." By now I began to feel really excited too.

The next day at one o'clock we left Aiken, Lucy and myself in front and Mr. Robbins in the back with open maps, all set to direct the traffic, as usual. Unfortunately, his directions were not successful because he was gazing at Lucy more than he was watching the roads. As a result we reached Macon way after four o'clock. The beauty of that town, with its enchanting old houses and Civil War atmosphere, turned us away for a while from the rather annoying feeling that we were late. Lucy powdered her nose and seemed very nervous. Driving out of Macon we began carefully looking for the presidential car. Nothing in sight. We drove for quite a while.

"Nobody loves us, nobody cares for us," sighed Lucy in a joking fashion, but I felt she was really disappointed. We were already approaching Warm Springs. It was a beautiful evening and the sun was beginning to set. As we entered Greenville, a village near Warm Springs, we suddenly noticed, by a corner drugstore, several cars and quite a crowd gathered around them. We drove up and there in an open car was FDR himself, in his Navy cape, drinking Coca-Cola! We pulled to the curb. Lucy and I got out of the car. The expression of joy on FDR's face upon seeing Lucy made all the more striking the change I saw in him since I painted him in 1943. My first thought was: how could I make a portrait of such a sick man? His face was gray and he looked to me much like President Wilson in his last years.

We were invited into his car, so Margaret Suckley, his cousin, and Fala, his famous Scottie, moved to the front seat. We started off, followed by the Secret Service men, with Mr. Robbins in my car closing the procession. In the excitement I had forgotten to take my coat and shivered all the way, while Lucy, seated next to the president and his Navy cape, was warm and happy. FDR said that he had gone to Macon, but after waiting awhile decided to make one more attempt at meeting us and went to the village close by.

There was an atmosphere about this drive that I will never

forget, Margaret Suckley and Fala in front and the three of us in the back. I did not listen to what FDR and Lucy were saying but tried to concentrate instead on the beauty of the crisp April evening and the lovely scenery that stretched before us. It was exciting and exhilarating. Finally the car stopped before the Little White House. I turned away when the body-guards carried FDR into the house. There was something so pathetic about his disability, particularly that night!

We were taken to the guest cottage, which was about a hundred feet away from the Little White House and consisted of two rooms. Mine was charming and had a rustic air. It was decorated with reddish toile, with plenty of prints and objects reflecting the president's interest in boats. Lucy's room was light with flowered chintz. We hurried to improve our appearances before a rather late dinner.

In the big room which served as a combination living/dining room and the president's office, FDR was seated by the fireplace in front of a card table he generally used for his work but was now turned into a bar. An old-fashioned was most welcome to me, particularly in anticipation of a pleasant evening in a charming setting and the most interesting company of the president, Lucy, Miss Suckley, and another of FDR's cousins, Laura Delano.

The latter, with bright blue hair, striking dinner pajamas, and a profile as beautiful as a cameo, was the only rather exotic looking person that night.

As usual, in the presence of FDR you experienced that feeling of complete ease and relaxation. He was full of jokes. I joined in the conversation, asking about the distance between Aiken and Macon. FDR laughed and said it reminded him of a recent remark from Churchill, "Let's not falter twixt Malta and Yalta!"

From Churchill the conversation shifted to his trip to Yalta and continued on the same subject through the dinner. "I was giving a banquet for the king of Saudi Arabia," began FDR, "and you cannot drink or smoke in his presence, according to Eastern etiquette. So I called up Winnie to remind him to have his drinks before, which he promptly forgot. At the dinner table, realizing this, he proceeded to sulk through the whole evening, just like this," and FDR made an amusing imitation of Churchill's expression. "The idea of the banquet was to exchange friendly bows with the sultan, who controlled great quantities of oil, and surely Churchill's attitude was of no help. At ten o'clock the sultan started to bid farewell. He had hardly left with his entourage when Winnie was already pouring Scotch into a glass!"

I asked if vodka was served at Yalta. "Oh yes, and I liked it very much. Stalin gave me a whole case, which I have in Washington, and also caviar which I brought here. It will be served tomorrow."

"Did you like Stalin?" I asked.

"Yes, he was quite a jolly fellow. But I am convinced he poisoned his wife! They seemed to be quite a nice crowd of people, except for a few sinister faces appearing here and there."

I was rather amazed that he uttered this remark about Stalin, but I realized that he really felt that none of those present would repeat anything he said. He spoke of the devastation of Sevastopol and Yalta by the Germans. The Imperial Palace of Livadia, where he stayed, had been completely stripped of furniture with the exception of a few monumental pieces that could not be moved, like the bed on which he slept, and pieces of early Grand Rapids type that did not match at all, these having been added to complete the furnishings.

"And how about the food?"

"It was typically hotel stuff, with a few exceptions. I was rather surprised at that because I have always heard of the lavishness of the Soviet receptions."

After dinner we moved from the dining area and sat chattering around the fireplace until Dr Howard Bruenn, the physician who had accompanied the president, came with his assistant. Before parting the president said he would be ready for me at twelve the next morning. Lucy and I retired to our cottage, and, being exhausted after the long drive and all the excitement, collapsed immediately on our beds.

In the morning, Lizzie, the maid, brought in our breakfast and it was only then that we really began exchanging our first impressions. I had moved with my tray into Lucy's room, where I established myself on the other twin bed. Lucy expressed her concern about the way the president looked, and about the fact that—except for Dr. Bruenn, a heart specialist, who checked the president's condition daily and was always on call—there was apparently no one with medical training to be in constant attendance on him. Frankly, I was more concerned about what I was going to do with my painting.

Many years before, a friend had introduced me to the *Daily Word,* a religious magazine containing articles and inspirational messages. Somehow, whenever I read the day's "word," it always seemed appropriate to that particular day. It certainly was the right one that morning: "By knowing God as our instant and unfailing help we can receive any idea, any counsel, any guidance when we need it." I read it to Lucy, since she knew how I relied on the help from above in my work, and understood me. We were still chatting when Margaret Suckley, with Fala, arrived to pay us a short morning call.

Much as I disliked hurrying, I was ready with my pencils and boards way before noon. My mind was blank as far as ideas for the portrait and, as usual, putting everything in God's hands, I was completely undisturbed. Upon entering the sunny room in the Little White House exactly at twelve o'clock, I was surprised to find it unoccupied. The card table the president had used the night before was covered with papers and the armchair was there, but no FDR. The doors to the porch were opened wide, and stepping outside I discovered everyone to be out there.

"We thought this location might be better for your painting," said Miss Tully after we exchanged morning greetings. I expressed no enthusiasm for it—I never painted outdoors, the lighting with no shadows being completely wrong. But looking at the president, who was sitting in a comfortable armchair, gay and at ease, I did not have the heart to move him inside. I will try it anyway, I thought, but if it had not been for that moment of weakness I could have done much more, later, on the portrait itself. Without actually repeating the 1943 portrait, I felt definitely that the famous cape should be introduced. FDR looked so thin and his gray suit hung loosely on his crippled body. The cape was brought in and ideas began to formulate. He got into a good pose, with the folds of the cape around him, yet the position of the left arm, dropping limply from the arm of the chair seemed meaningless, so I suggested his holding something, possibly a book. The president took a program of the Jefferson Dinner, with my 1943 portrait on the cover. That Jefferson Dinner was to be held on April 13 and the president was working on what was to be his last speech, ending with the famous words: "to you, and to all Americans . . . I say: The only limit to our realization of tomorrow will be our doubts of today. Let us move forward with strong and active faith." The program was just the right size, so we rolled it up and it looked fine. Somebody suggested that it would signify the peace treaty. "Oh no," said the president, "the United Nations Charter!"—that being most on his mind just then. He was planning shortly to attend the conference in San Francisco that would draft the charter.

After I had the position all settled, Mr. Robbins was brought in and made a few snaps. He was more nervous than usual, while the president continued joking with Lucy, who was sitting close by. I had not much time for sketching that day but was most optimistic about the outcome. At that moment, Mr. McCarthy, the former minister to Canada, arrived for luncheon. He had a most pleasing personality, plus a handsome appearance. I learned later that his son had been stricken with polio and that they were living in a nearby cottage at the foundation. We discussed with him the decision to have the president hold a scroll for the portrait. He also agreed that it was a grand idea. We went gaily into the house for luncheon. This meal turned out to be the longest of any in Warm Springs as the president continued talking indefinitely after the dessert, and some very interesting subjects were discussed.

At the time I felt I should be quite discreet about the things that I heard. The question of the war was the main topic and the optimistic attitude of FDR surprised me indeed. "It might end almost any time," he said.

As I think back on it now, I wonder why I did not then remember a strange statement made to me over the telephone just before leaving for Warm Springs. It came from a woman I had known for many years, who always seemed to have advance information about people and events, the source of which was clouded in mystery, but I suspected an astrological basis. For instance, she informed me of FDR's trip to Casablanca about a week before anyone else knew. Shortly before I left for Warm Springs, I asked her the question that was uppermost in the minds of all: "When will the war end?" Without hesitation she answered, "In about a month, and so will the president." But when, on April 10, FDR said that the war might end any time, I did not recall her prophecy.

Laura Delano asked, "What about Japan?" The question seemed definitely not diplomatic. The president exchanged smiles with Mr. McCarthy. "When the European war ends, Japan will collapse almost immediately." This was certainly a most surprising and heartening statement. We could hardly have guessed, at the time, that the president had the atom bomb in mind!

In the afternoon I continued making sketches for the background of the portrait in the cottage with Lucy watching. The pose was decided upon, but not the background. The portrait was to be life-size. I made one sketch with a plain background, another with some landscape resembling the surroundings at Hyde Park, still another with dark clouds which was quite effective. When Lucy, Laura Delano, and Margaret Suckley came in to see me and looked at the sketches, the plain background was unanimously approved. I showed this to the president before he left for a drive with Lucy and one of his cousins. She also thought the plain background best, though for a moment the suggestion of Hyde Park intrigued the president.

When everyone left I went for a walk in the woods where white and yellow azaleas were spreading their fragrance through the cool sunny atmosphere of the spring afternoon. There were sentries on duty at several places, but this did not distract me from the strange, almost dreamlike quality of the day.

When we gathered for cocktails, the president was again mixing drinks, with all the paraphernalia on the card table. I believe he really enjoyed being a bartender and he certainly was very good.

A pleasant dinner followed, though it was not very exciting as far as food was concerned. FDR retired rather early. Lucy and I went for a little stroll down the main road. Lucy chattered enthusiastically about the happenings of the day, and the only thing that seemed to disturb her was the fact that the president was really not well and that there was not enough attention directed toward his health.

"He really should have a male nurse or somebody to take care of him. He has an excellent doctor but that is not enough. His general health has been failing ever since his last campaign. He did entirely too much but he felt that he could not leave his post at that time." Repeatedly she mentioned her concern for his health.

She then told about his visit to Allamuchy during his last campaign, when he came to express his sympathy after Mr. Rutherfurd's death. Of course, this visit was never mentioned in print except for a few lines later written in Jonathan Daniels's *Washington Quadrille*. When she described how many people witnessed his visit, I expressed surprise that it never leaked through. Lucy thought it was quite natural. It was not clear to me how long he stayed at her home, but apparently it was long enough to have had a telephone installed for foreign calls. She said that a conversation with Churchill was the most exciting.

When we ended our evening walk, Lucy still did not wish to retire. I went to bed, but I could hear her for a long time moving about her room.

In the morning at breakfast Lucy showed me a photograph that the president had given her the day before. It was taken at the time when he was assistant secretary of the navy. She drew my attention to the scroll of paper he was holding, which was very similar to the one I was planning for the portrait. As we looked at the picture, Lucy began recalling old memories. She had never talked to me about the time she first met Roosevelt, and even now she was rather vague and reserved. I gathered, from what she said, that she first met him when he occupied the post of assistant secretary of the navy and she had a job in Washington, the details of which she never divulged to me. From the very beginning, there was a strong feeling of mutual admiration and affection between them. Inexorably drawn to each other, this feeling became increasingly intense and, in view of the fact that Franklin was married and had five children and Lucy herself was a strict Catholic, she knew that they must part since she could not consider a divorce. And they did, each going their separate ways. Lucy married Winthrop Rutherfurd and dedicated her life to her new family.

Only once during the lifetime of Mr. Rutherfurd, as she said, did she officially appear at the White House. This was when FDR was desperately sick with, I believe, pneumonia. She did not mention that there were any other meetings before her husband died. This particular meeting was at the request of Franklin Roosevelt, with the consent of Mrs. Roosevelt, and not only sanctioned, but urged by Mr. Rutherfurd himself. She did not go into detail but I felt the dramatic impact this meeting must have borne. As I looked at Lucy's beautiful, slightly flushed face and the picture of the handsome young Roosevelt in her hands, I was deeply moved by her story. And now they were together again in Warm Springs! The quiet and beauty of the place, the privacy of the surroundings, seemed almost created for the new blossoming of those old memories and I felt happy for them both.

But my mind was still preoccupied with the portrait I had

to paint. My little morning message, which I read again to Lucy, lifted my spirits. It said that I had to use every talent I possessed to the glory of God and the honor of man.

As Lucy and I continued talking, Mr. Robbins came in with his snaps. They were terrible, as I expected, and I decided I would have to beg the president to pose for another set.

At twelve o'clock I came in for my painting. The president was most cooperative, as usual, and agreed to be photographed again. I had one pose with the cape and another without, just as an extra picture for myself. Roosevelt was joking again with the photographer and Lucy. Then Mr. Robbins asked Lucy to pose, as he was anxious to have her picture too, on the same background. Lucy very sweetly obliged. Little did we know that these would be the very last photographs ever taken of him.

Before luncheon I hastened to put in a call to Pittsburgh to speak with my brother about the portrait. It was then I learned that he had been stricken with a heart attack. At luncheon the president expressed great concern for my brother's welfare and asked me to tell him to take good care of himself.

In the afternoon I began preparing my watercolor board and blocking in the portrait in full size, with the help of the photograph. At four o'clock the president left for his usual drive, and this time Lucy alone accompanied him. She told me upon her return that they drove to a favorite spot overlooking a view of the valley that Roosevelt particularly liked and sat there on a log. She said they had a most wonderful talk and the president spoke about world affairs, the past, and the future in the most inspiring way. She appeared deeply moved but did not go into any details of the last private conversation they ever had, and even later when she again mentioned their talk, she never disclosed anything about the past more than the vague statement she first made to me. She did add that tomorrow he was planning to drive her himself in the little Ford, but that tomorrow never came.

There was some excitement before dinner, as we learned that Henry Morgenthau, Jr., the secretary of the treasury, had arrived by plane. We were called for cocktails and I went first. I was a little embarrassed to find only Roosevelt and Morgenthau in the room, apparently in deep conference. I apologized and left, wondering what it was all about. In a short time when I reappeared with Lucy, the cousins were there and Roosevelt was again acting as bartender behind the card table.

I noticed that Morgenthau glanced at me without enthusiasm, and I suppose it was reciprocal. Maybe because through studying human expressions I have become very aware of different moods expressed or even concealed on human faces, I felt very strongly that he was preoccupied with something quite disturbing. He later made a telephone call, the reason for which, the president said, was his wife's illness.

A big bowl of Stalin's caviar, mentioned by the president on the first night, was served and it was really good. But there was an encompassing tension, partly due to Morgenthau's presence but also due to the anxiety of the president who had just talked with his daughter Anna, whose little boy was very sick.

Lucy always sat on the president's right, and he seemed constantly to address himself to her. She was looking particularly happy and animated that night. I recall that the dinner itself was unusually tasteless, dry meat balls and waffles with thick chocolate sauce for dessert. The conversation, however, picked up momentum as Roosevelt and Morgenthau began recalling different amusing and entertaining incidents about Churchill.

FDR at Warm Springs, April 11, 1945
(last photo)

Lucy Rutherfurd at Warm Springs, April 11, 1945

Morgenthau left immediately after dinner and the atmosphere resumed its former easy and pleasant manner. We all took our seats around the fireplace, with the president sitting comfortably in his armchair. Somebody suggested telling stories with a spooky background. Having a whole collection of ghost stories, I volunteered to tell one, and began one of my favorite narratives about the black pearl necklace of Catherine the Great. The president listened with that particular expression of complete attention he always gave to those who talked to him. Upon finishing my story, another was about to be told when Dr. Bruenn and his assistant arrived. The president, like a little boy, asked to stay up longer, but finally consented to retire, telling me that he would be ready for my painting the next morning.

Lucy and I returned to the cottage and our separate rooms. My impression was that Lucy went to bed late and got up very early. At breakfast, which we again had on our trays in her room, she told me she had hardly slept at all. She could not explain why but said that she had lain awake practically the entire night. Perhaps it was their last conversation, perhaps a premonition of what was going to happen. Once more, Lucy expressed her concern about the president's health. I did not read to her the *Daily Word* message, but on that beautiful spring morning, I pondered over it and wondered what it meant. It said that if circumstances look foreboding, if events seem to follow a course that could be disastrous to my best interests, I should have no fear.

Thinking about that day, April 12, 1945, I feel a great responsibility to tell exactly what happened. In the many later accounts, there were some discrepancies, but after all, there were only three other people in the room when the president was stricken. I am glad that I wrote it all down. My brother was the one, particularly, who urged me to do it. "Don't wait too long," he said jokingly, "because, remember, as the years pass by, the memory sharpens!"

I was in no mood to paint that morning. Even though I knew that the condition of my brother was improving, I was very anxious. I began collecting my easel and board but I did not take them with me when, at the appointed hour, I went to the Little White House. The president was seated, signing papers that Mr. Hassett was placing before him. I was so unwilling to paint that I suggested to the president that, if he was very busy, we could postpone the sitting until tomorrow. I knew it was going to be a full day for him. There was to be a barbecue that afternoon, given by the mayor of Warm Springs, and something else later. In talking about it the day before, the president had pleaded to stay in his car during the party but the general opinion being to the contrary, he meekly agreed to leave the car. It was clear that he suffered pain from his braces.

To my suggestion that we postpone the sitting, the president said, "Oh no, I'll be through in a few moments and will be ready for you." He looked cheerful and full of pep. I never realized, at the time, that Mr. Hassett was irritated by my presence. From what he wrote later on, he implied that I was a nuisance, that I was measuring the president's nose, which I *never* do, but fundamentally he was concerned that I was tiring the president with my painting.

Rather reluctantly I returned to the cottage and picked up my easel, paint box, and board. When I came back, Mr. Hassett was waiting for the signed papers to dry. They were all over the room, on every chair and table, his "laundry" as the president called it.

I placed my easel near the open door to the porch, with the

light to my left and the table with my paints and glass of water to my right. (If I'd only known how all this would be in my way a short while later!) The president was already seated in the designated spot with the card table· before him, covered with papers, mail that he was planning to look through. As I started mixing my paint, I looked very carefully at his face. I was struck by his exceptionally good color. That gray look had disappeared. (I was told later by doctors that this was caused by the approaching cerebral hemorrhage.)

Much later on, when I visited Lizzie, the maid, in Atlanta, she told me that the president was in a very good mood that morning. While he was having breakfast, he heard laughter from the pantry and asked what it was all about. Apparently the Filipino butler had overheard my ghost story of the night before regarding reincarnation, and being a believer in it himself, he asked Lizzie what she would like to be in her next incarnation. "A canary bird," Lizzie said, and because the enchanting Lizzie was extremely fat and heavyset, this created great laughter. And when the president heard it, he had a hearty laugh himself.

I began working with intense speed, with Lucy and Margaret Suckley sitting on the sofa at the other end of the room, talking and sometimes exchanging remarks with FDR. I began putting on the first coat of paint and then started, as usual, with the eyes. For this, I had to draw his attention from the papers, so I started a conversation about stamps. I had sent letters to my family that morning and was quite interested in the new Florida three-hundredth anniversary stamp and told him about it. I asked him if he, in any way, participated in the design of that stamp and he said that he did, and added, "Wait 'til you see the new San Francisco stamp, with the United Nations." He was looking forward to seeing it, and I understood how interested he was in this whole project. I felt an even greater responsibility regarding the portrait with the president holding what symbolized the United Nations Charter. I realized now why he had asked me to come at this time to paint his portrait and to finish it before the San Francisco conference.

In a little while, the eyes were placed and a familiar expression began to show. But it was not quite the look I was accustomed to during the past few days. The president seemed so absorbed, with the papers or something else, that when he would look up at my request, his gaze had a faraway aspect and was completely solemn. He brightened up when several times Lucy and Margaret Suckley exchanged remarks about the afternoon's activities. Laura Delano came in for a few minutes with her dog, Sister. Soon after, Margaret brought in a small bowl of gruel, for which the president showed no enthusiasm. Prior to this he had been given a small glass filled with green medicine. Looking at the unpleasant, bilious color, I asked what this medicine was for and was told "to increase the appetite." I remembered one occasion when Roosevelt had said that lately nothing tasted good and I thought to myself that if the green medicine was a remedy for lack of appetite, certainly that gray porridge before lunch would take every trace of it away!

At that moment the Filipino butler entered and began setting the table. The president glanced at him and said, "We have fifteen minutes more to work." As I remember, those were the last words he uttered. After that he became increasingly absorbed in his papers. Not wishing to disturb him, I continued painting the upper part of his face near the hairline. Suddenly he raised his right hand and passed it over his forehead several times in a strange jerky way, without emitting a sound, his head bending slightly forward. I never heard him say anything about a headache as was reported often in other descriptions of his last moments. Lucy and Margaret, sitting on the sofa, were continuing their conversation in quiet voices oblivious to what was happening.

"Lucy, Lucy," I gasped, "something has happened!" Within seconds Lucy and Margaret were on their feet. I pushed all my painting equipment to one side. Meanwhile, the president had collapsed unconscious in his armchair.

"Call the doctor, quick," somebody said. I ran outside where all the cars with the Secret Service men were usually stationed, but it was lunch hour and only one guard remained. "The president is sick, call the doctor!" I cried.

The guard did not seem to understand. I repeated my plea and ran back. Entering the hall I had my last glance of President Roosevelt, being carried to his room. I could not see exactly who was carrying him but I will never forget that silhouette on the background of the open door to the sunny porch. I just stood motionless for a moment, then entered the empty living room and quickly began picking up the portrait and my easel and painting equipment. The confusion was so great I hardly knew what was happening during those first dreadful moments. The doctor could not be located right away as he was at luncheon. Meanwhile the Secret Service cars began crowding the space before the Little White House. Servants were dashing back and forth. Miss Tully arrived and at last the doctor. He rushed to the president's room and in a short while returned. I was standing in the hall trying to put my easel together and get all of my things out of the way. I happened to be right near the telephone when Dr. Bruenn put in his call to Dr. Ross T. McIntire, Roosevelt's personal physician.

"He was quite well when I left him this morning," the doctor began in a hurried, nervous voice. "He complained of a slight pain in his neck but now something very acute has happened, sir." I heard no more of the conversation for I hastened to remove my things and leave the house. When I returned, Lucy and the others were standing in the living room and nobody seemed to know whether they were coming or going. I suddenly heard a strange sound. At first I thought it was the dog, Sister, who habitually snored in her sleep. Then I realized the sound was coming from President Roosevelt's room. I knew the end was near.

"We must pack and go," I suddenly heard Lucy's voice saying. "The family is arriving by plane and the rooms must be vacant. We must get to Aiken before dark."

In a few moments we were in the cottage, hurriedly tossing our things into suitcases. Lizzie was weeping as she helped us. As I was packing the unfinished portrait, she had a first look at it and wept even more. Margaret came to my room in tears and said something about last night's ghost story, the significance of which I did not grasp. From the window I saw an army car arriving with Mr. Robbins. One of the Secret Service men directed him away from the main entrance to the other side of the cottage. Our baggage was carried out. Miss Tully accompanied us to my car. Her eyes were red and swollen. She looked very different from the usually composed and perfectly groomed Miss Tully I was accustomed to. Mr. Robbins gazed at us in complete bewilderment, not daring to utter a word. The three of us got into my car. I took the wheel and slowly, hardly seeing where I was driving, we left the Little White House under a dark cloud of sorrow and distress. It was about two-thirty in the afternoon.

For a few miles we drove in complete silence, Lucy wiping

her eyes from time to time with a handkerchief. When we passed through the village where the president had met us, Lucy turned around and asked the location of that particular corner. Mr. Robbins pointed it out to her. He was still in a fog. And because the final issue of the president's collapse was yet uncertain, it was decided that we should not inform him about anything that had happened that morning. Lucy thought it would be best to give him, as a reason for our sudden departure, the excuse that she had received bad news about her eldest stepson, who had actually been wounded at that time.

As we approached Macon we noticed the flag at half-mast. "Somebody of importance must have died here," I said. Upon reaching Macon, Lucy was anxious to telephone her home in Aiken and, of course, Warm Springs. We pulled up before a big hotel on Main Street. Lucy got her call through to her daughter but all the lines to Warm Springs were unavailable. After several futile attempts, I suggested going upstairs to the main switchboard and asking one of the operators to try to make a special call for her. I went upstairs, entered the telephone office, and saw two operators—girls, weeping. "The president is dead!" one of them said.

The blunt statement came like a shock, even though I had just been in the midst of it all. I rushed back to Lucy who was sitting in the lobby waiting for me. She sat motionless and remained utterly silent. But the expression I saw on her pale face was more eloquent than words.

Mr. Robbins, who all this time had been trying to park the car in the crowded street, came in just then and I whispered to him, "He is dead." He thought I was speaking of Lucy's son and was full of sympathy. Silently we came out, and continued our drive in silence.

"Let's turn on the radio," Lucy said suddenly. I tuned in,

and the voice of H. V. Kaltenborn, the news commentator, came over the air. He was telling all about the president's death. I suddenly heard: "An architect was making sketches at the time of his death." An architect! Here it comes, I thought, shuddering. My name will be flashed all over the world! And I realized, with horror, what publicity was now awaiting me. All my life I'd disliked and shunned it. So far I had happily escaped it, in spite of the fact that I had painted numbers of prominent people, Roosevelt included.

"What?" Out of the blue came a cry from Mr. Robbins. "Why didn't you tell me?"

"We were especially requested not to mention anything until the end was certain," I said, trying to be as calm as possible since Mr. Robbins had a weak heart and had suffered an attack a few years before. Another collapse would be too much. I continued driving and Lucy began to talk, but I hardly knew what she was saying. I felt limp and finally asked Mr. Robbins to drive. Lucy and I sat in back discussing, among other things, the few mistakes we had made en route to Warm Springs. Well, we made even more on our way back. It was getting quite dark when we discovered that we were driving in a completely wrong direction, heading for Savannah, Georgia. We were forced to drive eighty miles further in order to reach Aiken. At last, after midnight, we arrived. Lucy's daughter awaited us and was certainly in a state! We hurried into Lucy's house. I had two calls, one from Pittsburgh and one from Locust Valley. Knowing that my brother was ill and how dangerous all this news would be for him, I decided not to call him at this late hour. But I put in the call to Locust Valley and in a moment my daughter Zoric was on the other end of the wire. She was quite excited and said that the latest news broadcast stated that when the president collapsed a Russian artist by the name of Robbins was painting his portrait!

It was wonderful to have a good laugh after all the gloom. And laugh we did, even Lucy joined in. I slept soundly and was awakened by a call from my brother. In the midst of the tragedy, he too was hilarious over the name of Robbins being mentioned. "We will have to call him 'Rubens' instead of 'Robbins' from now on!" It was wonderful to hear my brother, in spite of his condition, joking in his usual way! And I was so happy that *my* name had not been broadcast. At least not yet.

Of course nobody bothered us in Aiken as it was a complete secret that Lucy had accompanied me to Warm Springs. I believe the only people who knew were Mr. and Mrs. George Mead, her good friends in Aiken, and who later became mine. I decided to leave as soon as possible. I wanted to get home, and I began to feel panicky about the publicity I knew must be on its way.

As Mr. Robbins and I drove north, I became more and more depressed, obstinately refusing to tune in the radio or to buy newspapers along the way. All I wanted was to arrive unnoticed and unrecognized in dear Locust Valley. My heart was aching for Lucy, I was deeply distressed by the president's death, and in such a state of shock that I actually felt numb. Mr. Robbins was so sweet and understanding, trying his best to comfort me.

At one point, driving in the dark, we were stopped at a railroad crossing by the funeral train carrying the president's remains to Washington. It was a strange and sinister coincidence. Finally, we were stopped by a state police car and asked to identify ourselves. Mr. Robbins was behind the wheel and the state trooper asked, "Are you Mr. Robbins, the artist?" Mr. Robbins bowed his head in silent acknowledgement while

I kept as quiet as a mouse. Without further word, the state trooper motioned us to drive on.

Finally, we decided to stop for the night in some unknown little town, at some antediluvian hotel. I was half asleep when a telephone call from Washington woke me up. It was Senator William Langer from North Dakota. I could not understand a word he said. All I got was that he wanted me to come to Washington the next day and give a report (I could not make out to whom) of what had happened in Warm Springs and that he was sending an escort to bring me there!

After having been stopped by the state trooper, I knew that we were the object of pursuit and our whereabouts could not be concealed. I remember that when I talked to my daughter from Aiken, she told me that she was being besieged by reporters inquiring about my whereabouts, about how long I had been in Warm Springs, and so on. She had called Steve Early, the president's press secretary, at the White House, asking what she should say. He told her not to say anything and asked her to tell me not to release any information before he had informed us further. I was absolutely frantic. I dressed and woke up Mr. Robbins.

"You cannot go [to Washington]," he insisted. I decided to call George Mead in Aiken and he said Senator Langer had no right to make such a request.

We decided to leave at the crack of dawn, which we did, feeling like two culprits! I can understand the suspicion that developed when nobody could find me. After all, I was a completely unknown artist, except to those whom I had painted, and they were, I am sure, delighted that so far I had never used their names for publicity. And, being a Russian made it worse—it suggested Stalin somehow lurking in the background. So anyway, we departed.

Everything would have been fine if Mr. Robbins hadn't decided, for some unknown reason, to stop on our way at his apartment in New York City, somewhere on the upper west side. And what did we see? Reporters with cars waiting for him!

Acting on first impulse, we turned the car, Mr. Robbins at the wheel, and fled! I looked back and the cars were pursuing us. It was like a mad movie. As we zigzagged through Harlem I did not know whether to cry or laugh. On the Triborough Bridge, we managed to wiggle out of the traffic and in this maneuvering, I fell in a heap on the floor. By this time I was laughing so that I could not stop. From there on, the reporters lost track of us and we arrived safely at Zoric's house.

My daughter told me that Locust Valley was buzzing with newspaper men, and something had to be done about it. I had never in my life faced any reporters, and the very thought of it made me sick. However, salvation was at hand. Zoric had a good friend, who later became mine too. Her name was Edith Hay. An extremely intelligent, spirited young woman, she had a real flair for anything connected with the press. Later on, she started a weekly newspaper, the *Locust Valley Leader,* that in years to come, became one of the outstanding newspapers of its kind on Long Island. I always called her the conscience of our community because of her fearless, outspoken policy regarding anything that needed to be brought into the public's eye. Later that night we asked her what to do. She contacted the representatives of all the papers who had been there and talked to the whole bunch, setting a press conference for ten o'clock the next day.

After a good night's rest, Zoric, Edith Hay, and I had a little conference of our own. It was no longer possible to obey Steve Early's instructions to say nothing until we heard from

Franklin D. Roosevelt, 1945

him, and a telephone conversation with Lucy produced the same conclusion. I was rather amazed at how naive Lucy was, thinking that her name would not be mentioned at all.

Anyway, before the time set for the conference, reenforced with positive thoughts, and, I must admit, a good old-fashioned, I was ready to face the press. Zoric's living room was crowded with men, but I felt comfortably at ease. I answered all the questions without revealing Lucy's name. It was not easy. I said that I had painted the president's first portrait on my own and the second one was a commission from FDR and remained unfinished. They all wanted to see it but I said, though it was in my possession, I did not wish to display it just now.

The following day the papers all over the country were flooded with reports about this interview and, to my horror, printed photographs of myself. The question was, "Will she finish the painting or not?" Of course, the portrait remained unfinished.

That closed the story for the time being. As far as Lucy's name was concerned, it did not come up again until much later. However, it will always remain in my heart as a beautiful memory of a lovely, gentle woman whose very presence brought a warm feeling to those who were privileged to be with her. And the romantic friendship of a person like herself with President Roosevelt only enhanced his image to me.

THE AFTERMATH

The next few weeks were a real nightmare. I was still in such a state of shock that I did not realize what an extraordinary ordeal I had been through. Here was the president of the United States, recently returned from a conference in Yalta, looking like a ghost, having his portrait painted by a generally unheard of artist, Russian besides, and then collapsing in the middle of the sitting. The news of his death went round and round the world, wherever people could be reached. I suddenly became the center of weird and suspicious curiosity. Everyone wanted to see the portrait and to interview me. But, having said all I could at the first press conference, I flatly refused to elaborate on the subject, and have never since had any more official statements to make. My family and friends certainly protected me from all that publicity, which I dreaded all my life. The thing I feared came upon me with a horrible bang and it took me a long time to get back into my shell—to my painting and peace of mind.

After the portrait on the cover of the New York *Daily News* magazine section on May 27, 1945, I was flooded with letters, different requests, and whatnot. I was amazed that I did not get one unpleasant letter. On the contrary, all the comments about the painting and the personality of FDR were enthusiastic, and some were extremely moving. I had offers to buy the picture, but I felt that it would be most inappropriate to consider any financial deal. I had no idea what to do with it and what should be its final destination. So it was safely tucked away in a New York storage warehouse where it remained for several years until I was approached by Mr. Charles F. Palmer, a great friend and admirer of Roosevelt, then chairman of the Little White House in Warm Springs.

My encounter with Mr. Palmer, or Chuck, was the beginning of a warm and lasting friendship. His particular interest was in cleaning up slums, and he wrote several books on that subject. He was devoted to Roosevelt, and the creation of a memorial to FDR in Warm Springs took most of his leisure time. He was a very elegant, distinguished looking man with a short grayish moustache, thick dark eyebrows, and piercing blue eyes. In Atlanta, where he and his wife Laura lived, he gave lovely dinner parties, being a connoisseur of everything that went with them. The gay times I had with him and Laura, a shy, retiring, and utterly charming woman, made my visits to Atlanta particularly delightful. And yet, in the midst of all that gaiety if the name of Roosevelt was mentioned, Chuck instantly became solemn and his voice and expression changed to great reverence because he really worshiped that man. But we did tease him about it.

Chuck suggested that I donate the Unfinished Portrait, as it was unofficially called, to the Little White House Commission, and I agreed. Of course I had to present it myself and naturally say a few appropriate words on that occasion. In this I was helped by Winthrop Rockefeller, who was an expert on public addresses (but had no particular admiration for Roosevelt). He kindly composed a short address for me. Soon after I delivered my speech in Warm Springs, I received, funnily enough, the one and only unpleasant letter. In that address FDR was mentioned as the savior of our country. Among other things, the writer angrily asked, "From what did he save us?"

After Roosevelt's death a number of books about him began to appear. Some of the authors got in touch with me with requests to give them various bits of information, but I always refused to collaborate with them. Grace Tully, in *F.D.R. My Boss* (1949), was the first to report that when I was painting the president on April 12, 1945, Lucy Rutherfurd was among those in the room. Unbelievably, her name had never been mentioned in print before. Shortly after that, one of Lucy's stepsons told me that Westbrook Pegler had telephoned him and was planning to get in touch with me. How awful, I thought.

Sure enough he called. His first question was, "What is all this about Mrs. Rutherfurd?"

"I don't know what you mean," I responded placidly.

"Oh yes you do, and I would like to interview you on that matter." There was no escaping. I told him I would have to let him know the day when I could do it. I asked my daughter Zoric to be present at the difficult interview. When Pegler called again, we arranged a meeting in my New York apartment. At that time his daily column in the *Journal-American* was like a vendetta against the past Roosevelt administration, with especially vitriolic attacks against Mrs. Roosevelt, who was once more active in public life. His aim seemed to be to destroy whatever aura existed in connection with the late president. Lucy had died a year or so before. She had been a very private person and my fear was that Pegler wanted to use information concerning Lucy in some unpleasant way.

Pegler lived in Arizona and I knew that he was well acquainted with a friend of mine, Isabella Greenway King, who had been a congresswoman from that state for many years and had also been a lifelong friend of Eleanor Roosevelt's. Mrs. King was one of the great ladies of her time. As Lucy was a woman of the same calibre, I decided that in discussing Lucy with Pegler, I would make as many allusions as possible to Mrs. King.

Pegler arrived in his most bristly mood. Here I must rely on my daughter's observations. She said that my opening remark was, "Mr. Pegler, where have you been? I have been expecting you all these years." I do not remember saying it; all I know is that I wanted to greet him as graciously as possible. Anyway, Zoric said that he deflated visibly.

The interview went very well. I immediately established the connection with Mrs. King and in general followed my plan of telling about Lucy by comparing her with Mrs. King whenever I could. Since my information must have made poor copy for his column, he presented the "Lucy situation" as a molehill that had been made into the proverbial mountain. That was a relief to me, and I hope to the Rutherfurd family.

Then in 1948 there appeared an absurd book entitled *The Strange Death of Franklin D. Roosevelt* by Emanuel Mann Josephson who insisted, among other things, that the Roosevelt who died in Warm Springs was not the real Roosevelt but a substitute. When he called up for an interview, I just could not resist seeing him. Both my daughters joined me, and we really had a hilarious time. He was trying to persuade us by showing some photographs that it was not the same face because some moles were missing!

There were many other rumors regarding the circumstances of Roosevelt's death, and I must admit that in a way there was a reason: lots of the happenings were not resolved at that time. One time, when I was staying at the River Club in New York City, where very often I paint some of my out-of-town portraits, I needed a big board for some sketches. So I took a taxi to an artists' supply store. The board was brought out and put in the car, forming a screen between the driver and me.

"Are you an artist?" he asked.

"Obviously. Look what's between us."

"What do you paint?"

"Portraits."

"That must be very difficult. How do you get them?"

"Well, sometimes people call me, or write me, or meet me."

"You must be pretty good or you must have painted some famous people."

"Yes, I have." To which I added, "I painted Roosevelt, for instance."

"Roosevelt?" exclaimed the taxi driver. "I had great admiration for him and I know every portrait that was painted."

"Well, I painted the one on the day he died."

Dead silence. We were turning from First Avenue onto East Fifty-second Street where the River Club is located.

Then he asked, "Why are you here?"

"What do you mean?"

"Well, it is common knowledge that the person who was painting Roosevelt the day he died was sent by Stalin to poison him. So why are you here?"

I was really stunned. Finally I said that if there were any truth in it I certainly would not be here and would not be a member of the River Club. We stopped at the entrance, and I don't remember giving him a tip.

As the years went on, with Chuck's inexhaustible energy, the Little White House became a shrine to FDR's memory. Thousands of people, admirers and nonadmirers, flocked to that lovely spot in Georgia. I had been there several times myself with Laura and Chuck and I always felt rather nostalgic when I saw the place again.

Once I was being driven from Atlanta to do some portraits in Columbus, Georgia, and the chauffeur turned to me saying, "We are very near Warm Springs. Would you like to see the Little White House?" I said, "Of course!" I thought it would be interesting to go there alone, as a tourist, without being escorted or asked for an autograph. We arrived at the gates. I put on my sunglasses and bought a ticket at the entrance booth. And here I was again, alone, in that familiar setting. It was late in the afternoon; the winter sun was beginning to set. No visitors were around. I stopped first at the guest cottage where Lucy and I stayed. The doors to our rooms were open but corded off. I peeked in. Everything was just the same. I left with a feeling of indescribable sadness. When I entered the Little White House, a guard met me and offered to show me the museum first, but I said that I would just like to see the interior of the house.

He looked at me quizzically. "Have you been here before?" "Yes," I said, "on different occasions." As we came into the big living room I saw my portrait on an easel, behind a cord, and near it the armchair in which Roosevelt posed. As I looked at the portrait, the guard proceeded to tell me the story of the painting. He was very correct about everything and even mentioned that it was done in watercolor, a very unusual medium for that size portrait. At the end he said, "Of course, Mrs. Shoumatoff is a very old lady now, but I understand she still paints." "Good for her!" I exclaimed, and left the Little White House feeling one hundred and two!

As the twenty-fifth anniversary of FDR's death approached, I was invited to be the main speaker at Warm Springs. This time I composed the address myself, and after trying it out on a tape recorder with friends and family, I decided to deliver it without notes. We arrived in Warm Springs with my daughter Elizabeth, who had accompanied me on several official occasions in Washington, and Edith Hay (now Mrs. Wyckoff), editor of the *Locust Valley Leader*, who had been so helpful to me twenty-five years ago. I saw a tremendous crowd seated in front of the Little White House. I noticed how few polio patients with crutches there were. It was explained to me later that with the invention of the Salk vaccine, every year there were fewer and fewer. I was escorted to the platform at the entrance of the house. There were Chuck, triumphant and happy, Grace Tully, still beautiful, Frank Allcorn, mayor of Warm Springs at the time, Graham Jackson, FDR's favorite black singer, and masses of photographers, Edith already in the midst of them.

I looked at the crowd. So many familiar and unfamiliar faces, my daughter smiling amongst them. I felt quite emotional. After I was ushered to the stand, I started by giving a brief account of what happened twenty-five years ago and ended by telling, as an artist who had painted him twice, my impression of Roosevelt. I said that what amazed me most during those hours I spent with him was the fact that never, at any time, was I conscious or aware that the man whom I was immortalizing with my brush was crippled in any way. His alertness, his energy, and interest in everything were always there. I concluded with these words: "It has been said that you cannot disable ability and you cannot discourage courage. Franklin Delano Roosevelt proved with his life that nothing is impossible, and that is the greatest heritage that he left to us all."

Index